# Praise for *Rookie Father*

"Kendall Smith's new book, *Rookie Father*, provides a treasure trove of helpful ideas for new fathers and old fathers alike. As someone who has done research on families and has been married for 44 years with 7 children and 20 grandchildren, I found the book provides the kind of advice that all fathers need as they try to navigate the challenges of being a husband and father."

—**Gibb Dyer, PhD, author of *The Family Edge* and academic director of the Ballard Center for Economic Self-Reliance in the Marriott School of Business**

"How can you be a great chef if you didn't grow up eating food? That's pretty much the question Kendall Smith answers in this book about fatherhood from the perspective of a guy who grew up without a dad. The trick is to gather information, study some good examples, and adopt a curious and optimistic outlook that allows you to grow. This book is a great place to start!"

—**Lenore Skenazy, founder of Free-Range Kids**

"First-time dads need *Rookie Father*! If you're one of the almost 20 million men out there who grew up without a dad of your own to teach you the guiding principles of being a good man and father, then you've just found the ultimate playbook to show you the way. *Rookie Father* checks all the important boxes by touching on everything from the importance of creating meaningful rituals with your kids to why it's so important to have a cohesive partnership with your spouse. And I love that the author uses his own experience as a child of divorce throughout the book to share his insights and give new dads permission to use the hard moments from their past to create a lasting legacy for the future. Giving this one to every new dad I know."

—**Lisa Sugarman, nationally syndicated columnist, radio show host, and author of** *How To Raise Perfectly Imperfect Kids And Be Ok With It* **and** *LIFE: It Is What It Is*


"Kendall Smith has given us a personal account of his life as a growing father. He is willing to learn from other fathers, willing to share regrets, willing to explore how to triage family difficulties, and best of all, how to keep living a fit and healthy life to have the energy and love to be very available to his child. His loving care is unmistakable as he shares how he has overcome the trials of his childhood with a major mission: to be the best, most loving father he can be.

As he reveals experiences about learning from his wife, his devotion to his marriage, and the joy he has in parenting together, he sets the tone for an emotionally written, easy-going, fatherly style that comes across in every chapter. If you're a new father looking to feel engaged with another new father, Kendall is your guy. He's supportive, personable, and gives you the feeling that what he's learned, he wants to share with you."

—**Laurie Hollman, PhD, psychoanalyst, award-winning author of the Parental Intelligence series,** *Playing with Baby: Research-Based Play to Bond with Your Baby from Birth to One Year*, **and** *Living with a Narcissist?*

"Kendall Smith knows the damaging impact of being raised without a father and the irreplaceable power of being one. He has focused squarely on what a new father needs to know, giving any new dad a jump-start on the most important responsibility he will ever have! What better gift for a new dad?"

—**Michael Byron Smith, author of *The Power of Dadhood:**
***How to Become the Father Your Child Needs***

"Kendall Smith's *Rookie Father* is a well-written, easily digestible mini-encyclopedia for new dads. He leaves no stone unturned when it comes to situations faced by first-time fathers—from all of the usual "how to handle the kid" issues, to supporting your exhausted wife, to long-term financial planning that will affect your child, to dealing with (mostly) well-meaning in-laws. Kendall speaks from his heart through his deeply felt personal experience. His style is fresh and direct. If you are a new dad or about to be one or you know someone who's 'expecting,' this book is the perfect resource."

—**Ben Bernstein, PhD, the author of *Stressed Out! For Parents:**
***How to be Calm, Confident & Focused***

"Kendall Smith helps new dads take the reins when it comes to saving money and managing their finances, and his advice is grounded in reality: he provides suggestions that are actionable. *Rookie Father* can help new dads to achieve their goals when it comes to home purchases, college savings, and retirement."

—**Sara Yogev, PhD, clinical psychologist and author of *A***
***Couple's Guide to Happy Retirement and Aging***

"Many young men grow up without fathers in their lives. How do you parent without an example? *Rookie Father* answers this question—and many more. The author's casual writing style invites the reader on a journey through fatherhood that is full of wisdom and insight. He shares his own story of growing up with divorce and encourages the reader to look forward and not to the past in creating meaningful relationships. The book take-away gives the reader permission to create positive parent-child memories and connections that will filter through generations to come."

—**Christy Monson, marriage & family therapist and the author of** *Family Talk and Finding Peace in Times of Tragedy*

"Kendall Smith has a candid, straightforward approach that demystifies many of the daunting aspects of fatherhood. I loved the way he shares struggles from his own life and turns his hard-earned wisdom into manageable, actionable solutions that help men navigate the adventure of fatherhood. Any new dad will find this to be a tremendously useful guide."

—**Pam Lobley, humor columnist and author of** *Why Can't We Just Play?*

# Rookie Father

## A Playbook for Men Experiencing
## FATHERHOOD
## for the First Time

KENDALL SMITH

Published by Familius LLC, www.familius.com
PO Box 1249 Reedley, Ca 93654.

Familius books are available at special discounts for bulk purchases, whether for
sales promotions or for family or corporate use. For more information,
email orders@familius.com.

Library of Congress Control Number: 2021938994

ISBN 978-1-64170-573-8
eISBN 978-1-64170-593-6

Printed in China

Edited by Laurie Duersch, Peg Sandkam, and Spencer Skeen
Cover design by Brooke Jorden
Book design by Brooke Jorden and Maggie Wickes

10 9 8 7 6 5 4 3 2 1

First Edition

Dedicated to my son, Connor.
I love you more than the stars love the sky.

# Acknowledgments

**W**hen I first heard the African proverb, it takes a village to raise a child, it hit a nerve. At that moment, I knew I had to give credit to the town of Ho-Ho-Kus, New Jersey, and their residents for having the patience to put up with my antics. There were times when neighborhood parents, teachers, Boy Scout leaders, and fellow grade schoolers had no idea how to manage a hyperactive adolescent with the attention span of a gnat. So many people made a positive impression in my upbringing that it's worth acknowledging some of them. They exuded a level of patience I cannot fully comprehend.

But first, I have to shower praise on my wife and best friend, Allison, who's been one hundred percent supportive, loving, and honest throughout our sixteen years of marriage. I'm proud of the life we've made for each other, our son, and our pets (Bowie and Trooper). I love you.

I also want to thank my agent, Anne Devlin, for taking me on as a client and introducing me to the fantastic people at Familius Publishing. I'm honored to be associated with such a wonderful publisher that reflects a mission I hold close to my heart—one that espouses love for family. I tip my hat to Christopher Robbins, Brooke Jorden, Kate Farrell, and everyone I've worked with to date. I'm excited to see where our shared journey takes us.

I appreciate the advice and counsel provided by Susan Schader and Shana Milkey, who both shared a fresh perspective while I revised *Rookie Father* over several years.

I would also be remiss not to thank the people who agreed to be interviewed and featured in *Rookie Father*: Alan Katz, Dana Glazer, and local parents, Mark and Steve. Your stories inspired me, and I'm sure readers of this book will find value in the wisdom you shared.

Credit is owed to the teachers of Ho-Ho-Kus Public School, who guided me during some very turbulent times when I experienced my parents' divorce and estrangement from my father.

Huge credit is owed to Mrs. Stenwall, who provided a gift to me upon my eighth grade graduation: a copy of The Next to Nothing Book. Within it she inscribed a note that encouraged me to continue writing; she saw something in me that no one else noticed. Thank you, Mrs. Stenwall, and I'm not done writing yet!

I also have to thank Mrs. Mardy, Mr. Catsos, Mr. Cushing, Mrs. Greenspan, Mr. Molzan, Dr. Woodbury, and all the other fantastic grade school teachers that provided me with encouragement and discipline.

One particular organization in my hometown made a huge impact in my life, and I credit their members for teaching me how to be more responsible and resourceful. To the leaders and members of Troop 54 in Ho-Ho-Kus, New Jersey . . . thank you. Mr. Stuhr, Fred Hauser, Steve Newton, and all the terrific scouts— you helped to fill a void in my life when my father was absent. You collectively prepared me for adulthood.

I also have to pay homage to the wonderful families in Ho-Ho-Kus who kept an eye on me, played a positive role in my upbringing, and managed to deal with a whirlwind of chaos that ensued when I played with their kids. And, of course, I have to thank the dads and moms in my hometown: The Hobbises,

Algeos, Winiarskis, Keivits, Johnsons, McVeys, Dohertys, Staniars, Moores, Autys, Reels, Madisons, Portsmores, Shafers, and dozens of others. Trust that the patience you exuded is something I try to emulate when I spend time with my son, his friends, and our neighbors.

Lastly, I have to acknowledge you, the reader. If you are like me and were raised in absence of a father and are doing everything you can to provide a better life for the next generation, you have my respect.

# Introduction

**W**hen you think about it, parenthood is true adulthood. Everything that comes before is a cakewalk compared to the moment when you are baptized as a father.

You're accountable 24/7 for the life of another human being. Whatever mischief you got yourself into in the past, whatever your present habits or hobbies, it all takes a backseat to your number one priority: your child.

As a kid from a divorced home and now a parent, the inspiration for this book centers on my experiences of growing up without a father. My foray into fatherhood came with a different set of tools, experiences, and overall wisdom. I had my mom, of course, and my grandmother as well to provide a framework of how to parent, but I also looked outside our family to understand what fatherhood really meant.

Allow me to share one example.

My best friend, Ricky, who lived four doors away, sat beside me as we watched our third hour of television (likely cartoons, as this was before the age of Nickelodeon) on a sunny and beautiful summer day. We vegetated on the couch like normal eight-year-olds, enjoying a lazy morning after I slept over at his house.

The door to the room burst open. Ricky's father stood over us.

"Hi, Mr. Johnson."

He ignored me as he glanced at the TV, looked toward the window where the sun was beaming, and then finally addressed us.

"What are you doing in here?" His voice rang out in a tone of deep concern.

"Watching TV, Dad," said Ricky.

"That's ridiculous. Look at the weather. It's gorgeous outside!"

"Yeah . . . so?" As soon as I said the words, his eyes glared at me with the accuracy of two lasers pointed straight at my skull.

"That's it! Now get outside. Enough of this TV. You should be playing in the backyard!"

He ushered us along and opened the door to the garage. The sun was so bright I had to cover my eyes. "Go . . . now!"

Our proverbial asses hit the back of the door as we exited, grumbling while we made our way to the driveway. Ricky and I threw a football around and took turns doing whatever eight-year-olds do. Sans a brief respite from the heat to enjoy lunch, we were outside all day and enjoyed ourselves. Other than when Ricky's mom gave us sandwiches, we didn't see his parents for the rest of the day.

When it was time for me to leave, I thanked the Johnsons for letting me sleep over and walked back to my house. On that walk, I thought about the day's encounter with Ricky's father, which had resulted in a great day of activity . . . outside . . . in the backyard . . . with lots of sunshine and fun. I also thought that the way Mr. Johnson reacted to our lethargy in front of the TV meant he really cared. I appreciated that.

These kinds of lessons set the tone of fatherhood for me.

At my house, it was just my mom and me. My father separated from my mother when I was six. When this occurred, he uprooted himself and moved to Florida. Despite receiving postcards, phone calls, mailed gifts, and seeing him twice a year on annual trips, I really missed my dad. Unlike Ricky, I didn't have a father and would remain without a regular father figure for the remainder of my life.

Before the episode at the Johnson's house, I experienced a number of situations that made me realize how much I was missing by not having a father in my life, an awareness that magnified as I got older. But especially after my experience with Mr. Johnson that sunny day, I paid extra close attention to other kids' fathers.

When I was in high school, the men who coached our local soccer teams organized a trip to Germany to participate in a soccer tournament. I was active in the sport and this opportunity was exciting. But then I learned it was a father/son soccer excursion, and I watched all my friends leave to play our favorite sport with their fathers in tow. This left a lasting impression. And things got worse for me.

Despite having the benefit of a strong, independent, and positive role model in my mother, the relationship I had with my father soured further when he cut off child support payments to my mom. From that point onward, he and I had an estranged relationship. A few letters were exchanged, and we saw each other once during my senior year of high school for a few hours when he came back to visit his relatives in New York. That was it. Having witnessed what my mother went through—almost losing our house to foreclosure, and my father's disinterest in my high school and college graduations—I wrote him out of my life. He passed away one year and one month prior to the birth of my son, Connor.

Throughout the years, I made myself a promise: If and when I became a dad, I would never let my son or daughter down. This became my singular mission. Psychologically, my goal was to turn my father's negatives into a positive for me and the next generation. Part of me hoped to right a wrong that had taken place in our family history; it would be the ultimate payback for what I went through as a child. And my father's grandson, Connor, would grow up with two loving and adoring parents from the moment of his birth until my last days in this world.

I also had something else in my arsenal I could use—all the fatherly lessons I learned by watching my friends and their dads, along with relatives who bestowed upon me important lessons about life. The early years of my marriage provided me with a foundation that made me appreciate the institution of marriage itself because I married a terrific woman whose parents have been married for over fifty-five years—an in-law bonus package.

And another life experience motivated me to write this book. As an adult, my travels provided a unique opportunity—one I did not take for granted or squander. I learned the value of wisdom and the benefits of procuring a broader knowledge base about life itself.

One day in March 2000, when I was halfway through a backpacking excursion that took me throughout Southeast Asia, the combination of intense heat, humidity, and a scorching sun drove me to enter a Buddhist wat (temple). The shade of the interior felt forty degrees cooler and my shirt was soaked through with sweat, and I found myself on the grounds of a large religious site in the heart of Bangkok.

I was relieved to find the grounds free of monks, whom I did not wish to disturb. A hundred or so tourists roamed the temple grounds, and I wanted to exude respect for the monks' faith, though my fellow travelers never failed to disappoint me. Their barren shoulders, rude behavior, and penchant for hookers and drugs represented a repeated pattern of behavior that contrasted with my pursuit for a cultural adventure in Southeast Asia. The trip was supposed to be my escape from becoming burnt out in the dot-com industry. I was twenty-nine years old, only one month into my journey, and in the middle of a life crisis.

Shortly after entering the wat, a Buddhist monk appeared from a side room and greeted me with a smile. I apologized for being there and begrudgingly made my way to the main door to reenter a city that seemed to be on fire. He motioned for me to stay and visit with him. He wanted to practice his English and invited me to talk for a while. If I had to guess, he was in his forties; based on what I knew about Buddhism, he had been a monk in saffron robes since his pre-teen days. Translated, he had been a practicing monk for at least thirty years.

His desire to practice his English provided me with an opportunity to learn more about Buddhism. This was an area of significant interest for me. I wanted to see if faith provided perspective on life and the challenges we face in the modern world.

He spent the next two hours explaining one of the core tenants of Buddhism: The root of human nature is anchored by the fact that we are all "suffering." The concept does not relate to physical pain, or even a religious principle. It is centered on dealing with the world, how we manage our choices, and the wisdom we possess (or not) to make sound decisions.

He spoke at length about *how* we make a decision, what we process, and the resulting judgments before we act. He broke it down into the simplest of examples: deciding whether or not to sit on a particular chair. We deduce, more often than not, on past decisions: one chooses to sit in the chair based on the faith that it can hold our weight.

Choosing whether or not to sit on a chair is pretty straightforward, but it does, in fact, represent a decision. But what about more complex choices? The higher up the decision food chain you go, things get more complicated and choices become more numerous.

How does this relate to suffering? We, as humans, are not born with infinite wisdom—that comes with time and experience. Thus, we are suffering on some level until we procure enough wisdom to make smarter decisions. It begs the question: Does one possess enough wisdom to make *correct* decisions?

My interpretation was that on some level exists a hierarchy of wisdom. There are those who pursue it and learn from their mistakes, and others who do not. Buddhism's focus is centered on trying to find the right path to reduce "suffering," and to make better decisions that do not result in upending or uprooting the broader community.

*The pursuit of wisdom* . . . that's what I took from my two-hour chat with the monk. He was pleasant, friendly, forthcoming, and truly helpful. My perspective prior to this trek was solely focused on earning a living through commissions and salary, which is not healthy. The trip itself, in hindsight, was a quest I pursued to see what else life had to offer. I left the temple that day valuing wisdom more than money, which is why I define this episode during my trip as a signature event.

So how does this story relate to *Rookie Father*? If this book provides you with the ability to make smarter choices, resolve one lingering conflict, reunite with one important person in your life, or provide a single guiding principle on how to be a better father, then its mission has been accomplished. It represents a playbook for men who, like me, did not have a regular and dependable father figure.

This work represents all the collective wisdom I've garnered, and I hope you find it useful, concise, and relevant. It does not represent a professional guidebook on the health and physical care of your child. Plenty of books cover those subjects. It is written for the 19.4 million men who grew up in a single-parent home or lost their father to divorce, estrangement, or untimely death.

This is about *your* role in the family. If you're like me and you did not have a day-to-day father figure, I hope you find more than a few chapters relevant and helpful.

Onwards and upwards,

**Kendall Smith**

# CONTENTS

**A NOTE ABOUT GENDER:**
You'll find some chapters mention "son" and others "daughter," which is used to vary the gender of a child from one chapter to the next. The advice provided does not pertain to any particular gender; it is intended for either or for children who are gender non-conforming. This approach is often used in parenting books to make it more personable and to avoid the overuse of the word "child" or "infant."

# PART 1

Setting Your Foundation

# CHAPTER 1

# Section Preview: Setting Your Foundation

**T**he moment your child is old enough to walk, don't be surprised if he comes running toward you every time you return home from work. If the roles are reversed and you're a stay-at-home dad, you'll witness this yourself with your spouse. It's the ultimate prize after a tough day of work or a lengthy commute: the perks of being a parent. No one wants to see you more than a child who has not seen you all day.

It's simply magical; the connection between parent and child is one of life's greatest gifts. If you grew up in a two-parent household, you can likely relate to this memory or experience.

Those of us who grew up in divorced households may have had to wait until the weekend to see a parent otherwise not seen during the workweek—often true in a country where the divorce rate remains stubbornly high at 50 percent. Some, like myself, had to wait four to six months if a parent lived far away. And others lost their connection with their father altogether.

There are those among us who grew up in single-parent households where memories linger of one parent leaving the home . . . permanently. I vividly recall the day my father left to move to Florida. I was six. Hugging and kissing my father goodbye as a taxi waited for him at the curb was heart-wrenching. No words can describe the moment when one of the two constants in my life disappeared. Knowing he would live two thousand miles away from us raised dozens of questions in my mind. To this day, I still don't have all the answers. It's like trying to piece together a document that's been run through a shredding machine.

That brings me to the purpose of this book: a "playbook" to provide a foundation for men who grew up without a father figure in their life. Finding inspirations from your youth, keeping your marriage in good shape, maintaining healthy family relationships, managing money, involving yourself with local institutions (and staying involved), and setting a foundation for a positive legacy are what I lean on when I think about the day my father left.

And I strive to achieve and succeed where he failed.

When my son dashes into my arms at night, one word comes to mind, and I hope you will embrace it as well: **consistency**. Being a consistent and positive force in the life of your child represents a gigantic step forward from one generation to the next. You can represent the light of your son or daughter's life, and in doing so, set a stronger foundation for the generations that come after you.

Which leads me to the first section—setting your foundation. The aim here is to reflect on yourself first, then build from there. I wish you all the success in the world during your journey as a successful father figure.

# CHAPTER 2
# The Beginning

The instant your child enters the world, a fire hits your soul and melts it. Nothing is like it. No experience in life can prepare you for that event, that emotional rise in pressure, the feeling of resurrection on some level that wipes the slate of your life's journey clean. It is pure, warming, and joyful. And once that first cry of life squeaks from the tiny mouth of your child, it represents a moment of pristine clarity.

I could not wipe the smile off my face until my head hit the pillow at 2:00 a.m. Even then, I think I smiled as I slept throughout the night. When I awoke, I was in a hotel room twenty miles north of the hospital where our birth mother and my wife shared a room with our son, Connor.

Shortly after our eight-and-a-half-pound baby entered the world, his length and weight surprised me. I came up with two nicknames within ten minutes: "Connor the Barbarian" and "Bam Bam." Connor the Barbarian stuck, and still does to this day.

What you felt in that moment when you were baptized a father is exactly what your father likely felt. Somewhere in between, life got tangled, complicated, confusing, and bewildering to the adults who were your parents. All parents face tests in their marriages and their family lives, and in many cases, those tests become harder as one ages.

Whatever flaws your parents had or were exacerbated in challenging times, make yourself one promise as a new dad: *rise to the moment.* Keep perspective and stay strong and resilient when it comes to your commitment to parenting and fatherhood. A concept you'll see in a later chapter, which I'll note here, is to devote yourself to raising a winner, no matter where you netted out with your education, income, or upbringing. If you leave this world giving your son or daughter a better chance than you had, and if you were a father in the truest sense of the word, you've passed the most important test life has bestowed upon you.

That is the true American dream at its core. Make your dreams a reality by committing to the task at hand.

# CHAPTER 3

# How Will You Parent?

**M**en who grew up with two parents often have a pre-established perspective on how they should parent their child. With regard to managing certain circumstances, the level of discipline to enforce, and priorities versus trivial challenges, the solutions that come to mind are part of the fabric of their childhood. And more often than not, their preconceived approach to parenting gets the job done.

Here's a unique perspective to consider that millions of men who did not grow up with fathers in their households share with one another: You have the opportunity to take a more independent route as a parent. You represent a clean slate without set boundaries of how a father should approach the ups and downs of parenting.

Did you grow up with a friend whose dad yelled at him when he misbehaved? Did you know a family during your childhood with a hot-tempered mother who ruled with an iron fist? What examples did you see growing up that stood out as negative examples when it came to parenting, regardless of gender?

Those examples may provide some guidance when you have to manage challenging situations. You can learn from the mistakes others made or (in the hot-tempered example noted previously) you can control your emotions when your son is misbehaving.

On some level, those negative examples can be liberating, freeing you to do the opposite. Telling your child you love them every day, or simply showing more affection than you received as a child, may represent a positive break from the past. Alternatively, you can be more involved in disciplining your child if you were given too many liberties and needed more boundaries set.

You can now set your own parental standards. Don't be afraid to embrace the opportunity.

# CHAPTER 4

# The Mission at Hand and Your Past

**Y**ou know your childhood better than anyone, and at some point during your first year as a father, you will reflect upon it. Your early memories may include some sharp (and perhaps painful) episodes—a common experience for those of us whose parents divorced. You may feel a real void in terms of what you missed given your father's absence if he divorced your mother or passed away when you were young.

At some point in life, the past creeps up and bites us on the keister when we least expect it. That's the problem (on some level) with the human experience. We tend to remember the very best and worst days throughout our lives.

When such moments arise, the first thing to do is embrace them. Call them times of reflection or moments of clarity. Don't deny or bury them—face them as challenges.

Second, keep one single word in mind when these moments occur: **trajectory**. If nothing else, keep the trajectory of your home, work, and family life on the upswing. If that requires night classes at some point, or setting a strict budget to afford tutoring for your child in middle school, do it. Make decisions with a sober mind and communicate consistently with your spouse to ensure you are both on the same page.

The net result will be a better childhood for your son or daughter, and all the children you bring into the world. That is all that matters. If you can position yourself to look back twenty years from now and say you did everything you could to provide a meaningful life for your child, you will have corrected a major imbalance in your family's lineage.

You have the power to make that happen.

That's a real accomplishment and more meaningful than any luxury or indulgence money can buy. Being able to say you "manned up" when it counted most is the greatest luxury one can procure.

# CHAPTER 5

# The Traps before You

**A**nother dimension may surface after you become a father. Sometimes bad habits pass down from one generation to the next. Whether it's smoking, drinking, a bad temper, or indifference to certain circumstances, you may experience anxiety if and when you have to address the issue.

Some men experience this at a deeper level—a self-inflicted perception that you will fail your child at some point. It may lurk in the back of the mind, empowered by the demons of one's youth from growing up with a father or mother who let them down.

It could represent an uncompromising desire—sex, a former addiction, or the fear your wife or intimate partner is likely to cheat on you.

It can seem like a trap, one waiting to spring open down the road later in life.

The positive side of this circumstance is you have the means to control your destiny, and it's something you should never forget. If your concerns arise again and again, you should feel no shame or concern about speaking to someone about it. If you are not comfortable addressing it with your wife or partner, find a therapist. Spend some time fleshing it out and get your emotions and concerns out on the table. An unbiased third party who has experience helping others with anxiety can help provide a roadmap to overcome this so called "trap."

You'll be shocked how good it feels to speak about and talk through the issue. And it will make your future seem that much brighter.

Hope, itself, is worth the time and investment.

# CHAPTER 6

# What Does Your Fatherhood Ultimately Mean?

Perhaps it simply means to give your daughter a great childhood, and a much better one than you had as a child.

If you experienced your parents telling you they were separating . . . or vividly recall the day your father passed away . . . or you never knew your father and were raised by a single mother . . . perhaps your role in this life is to give something back that you never had.

That's your distinction in this world, and you're making it a better place simply by passing along something to the next generation. That's honorable.

You come equipped with a perspective that other parents who came from two-parent families do not fully appreciate. It's something they take for granted or continue to rely on to this day. They have (or had) two parents when they were kids, parents who—despite their flaws and shortcomings—provided them with a basic foundation of support.

Today, you represent that bedrock of support for your daughter, and it is an honor and a privilege to give her a solid foundation. Frustrations will still arise and (let's be honest) you have your own shortcomings like anyone else; however, from day one of your child's life until you leave this world, you can consider yourself a success by every measure if you play an active and committed role.

A fantastic goal to aim for is to do everything you can to provide a stronger family foundation. That way you'll never have regrets, such as, "I should have been around more often when . . ." Reciprocally, your daughter will never say, "Daddy wasn't around when . . ."

The moment will come one day when you realize you provided a better life for the next generation. That's something to look forward to, so make it happen.

## CHAPTER 7
# Setting Your Foundation

**Y**ou may not have grown up with a father figure in your life. Let's get that out on the table. There are many like you in the world, including myself.

Read that first sentence again because, upon becoming a father, you have an important choice to make. You can go down the self-pity/victim path and tell yourself you are struggling to come to grips with the challenges you'll face as a new dad. There's no fault in this; in fact, it's rather progressive. At least you're thinking about how growing up without a father in your life could affect your ability to parent.

Guys who do not give *any* thought to the matter are, on some level, in denial. Being a father is no small thing, and unless you address the subject, eventually you will wonder if your shortcomings as a parent are connected to your father's absence. A man who goes through this cycle of self-doubt may end up second-guessing himself.

This can linger for months, even years . . . but then there's the other option, which is to find your own way.

But is there another alternative? A third path? Sorry, no dice. Can you do something for yourself that will give you a better chance to become a great dad? If you dig a little deeper, you'll be surprised by what you have to work with in terms of people who inspired and shaped your perspective of the world.

Of course, start with your mother; that's the easy answer. She was likely a major inspiration and an exceptional parent, but it's also worth thinking about other people who were role models in your life.

First, you have to look back across the years. Whether you're an orphan, the child of a deceased father, estranged from your dad, or have a strong distaste for the man who raised you, you can think back and rediscover other adults who helped guide you through life. It doesn't have to be a list made exclusively of men. Women can play a role, as well as close friends and community figures.

This is called "setting your foundation." It takes a little effort, but I guarantee you'll feel a lot more confident when you go through this process.

Take some time alone, separate from others, your job, and your spouse, and dive deep into your past to consider all the role models you've met in life. It can be anyone: a teacher who noticed and encouraged a talent you possessed; a Boy Scout troop leader who taught you what it meant to persevere; a childhood friend who fought through a horrible disease and survived to tell the tale. Consider other fathers who were part of your childhood and who set good examples and raised solid kids.

Even fictional TV characters may have struck a chord with you. Despite the crimes he committed, I personally found James Avery's character in *The Fresh Prince of Bel Aire*, Philip Banks, to be an excellent father figure when I was a kid. If someone who simply portrays a father provides you with some level of inspiration, embrace it. Keep track of those you most admired. It doesn't have to make sense to anyone but you.

Go one step further—what did those role models *represent*? What made them stand out in your mind? Write down a sentence or two next to each person's name. It may even prompt you to drop someone from the list. Keep focusing your thought process. Think about what else he or she did that affected you in a positive manner.

This helps you pinpoint certain traits, unique qualities, and positive attributes that influenced who you are.

Stand back and look at what you've written. This is not some self-serving exercise to exclusively serve your needs—it's about your son or daughter. Would you like your child to espouse the same values? If your child exuded these traits, would you be proud of him or her?

That, in essence, is the purpose of "setting a foundation" for yourself. It's a playbook for the values you want to pass down to your kids. I promise that once you start digging, you'll find a trove of people who helped guide you.

This process of setting a foundation for yourself can provide the opportunity to be an *outstanding* father. Growing up without a father figure can, in some cases, even provide you with an advantage—one that guys who have fathers cannot even begin to process.

Or you can sit there and feel bad for yourself. When in life did that ever help you get ahead?

## CHAPTER 8

# Gaining Altitude

**M**otion and lift are the two essential principles you need in order to fly, but the one thing that will prevent you from taking off is too much weight. Load up a single-prop plane with a few tons of baggage and you won't get anywhere. You'll careen down the runway, hit the brakes right before the end of the tarmac, and flip the plane on its backside.

If you're a new dad who experienced negative side effects while growing up, stemming from the absence of a positive father figure, it's time to lose some baggage. The word "baggage" in this context touches on a psychological term that relates to your family history, and it may influence your role as a father today. You likely incurred some emotional scars throughout your life. It's part of the human experience—everyone carries some form of "baggage."

When you look back in your life to find inspiring people who had a positive impact on your upbringing, consider another element. Think about the adults who did nothing to elevate you as a person, the sad souls who had bigger issues to deal with: a friend's mom who was emotionally disconnected, an absent father who came and left too frequently, or an adult you crossed paths with who drank during the day when he/she should have been acting like a responsible parent.

If you can still smell his/her breath, that represents baggage on some level, regardless if they were part of your immediate family or not. If you're still in touch with them or they play any role in your life, it's time to consider if they should be present in your child's life. If there's a lifelong friend or relative who pops up now and then and brings a cloud of irresponsibility with them, it may be time to keep relations with them at a distance.

It can be hard, but if you don't eliminate negative influences, that may be the equivalent of carrying unnecessary baggage—especially if you're a new dad and trying to gain altitude as a responsible and caring parent.

# CHAPTER 9

# The "Labor" of Expectations

**I**f you're three months or three weeks out from your wife going into labor, you need to discuss some truly basic (but essential) needs.

You will undoubtedly have multiple decisions and preparations to make, but touching on the core essentials may help alleviate some stress when you bring Junior home. This relates to Maslow's Hierarchy of Needs, with one notable addition (which I'll cite here as the first point in the list).

1. **Sleep.** Have you and your spouse discussed how you will manage feedings in the middle of the night? You have two choices: split the night in half, where one of you sleeps from 9 p.m. to 3 a.m. and the other handles the early morning hours; the other option involves alternating nights to ensure one of you gets a full night's rest. For couples where the mother breastfeeds (and you can't help with feedings), tackle everything you can for the baby before your wife and child nod off, and take over early in the a.m. whenever possible.

2. **Shelter.** Do you both agree that you will stay in your current location over the next year? If not, commit to staying or moving before your child is born. Moving is not easy, but prioritizing this will take the stress out of deciding whether or not to move.

3. **Food.** Decide who will do the grocery shopping and how you will manage dinner when you are all together

at night. Do you need to make a large meal on the weekend in order to have leftovers to eat during the week? Another suggestion worth discussing is to buy a slow cooker. It is one of the easiest ways to cook; the time to prep veggies and meats can be done in minutes, and once you turn on the slow cooker, the meal cooks itself. Having a complete and tasty meal ready to eat in six to ten hours is a Godsend when you're preoccupied with an infant.

4. **Clothing.** This represents the third official need in Maslow's hierarchy, but it's number four in this chapter. Kids grow out of clothes quickly and you and your wife can't ignore your own wardrobes. It's less important than the other three listed previously, but double-check to ensure you're setting aside money to afford new clothes so you're not stressing out later with unexpected expenses.

Having a game plan will reduce stress and it will put you and your spouse on the same page before Junior comes home.

# CHAPTER 10

# The Clock Ticks . . . But You Don't Know All the Tricks

If the enormity of becoming a father—and the anxiety that comes with it—seems a bit overwhelming, keep three things in mind:

First, tell yourself to take one day at a time. The foundation of time it takes to learn how to parent (properly) comes in small increments.

Second, open your mind and your heart to advice that will help you and your wife. Rely on your mom and mother-in-law, sisters or brothers, and especially older relatives who have experience as successful parents. Never be afraid to ask someone to share their wisdom.

Third, if something is not working, *revise and adapt*. If it's hard to burp your son after his bottle, perhaps he needs a different type of nipple. If something seems off with his development, discuss it with your wife and research steps you can take.

And if all else fails, the internet can provide relevant parental advice if you search in the right place. Stick to video interviews or articles from well-respected sources. Will Smith noted this years ago when he was interviewed during a daytime talk show. He shared the fact that today, the knowledge one needs is there for the taking, and if the source represents a trusted entity, it's worth considering.

The answers won't come all at once, and you can tackle one challenge at a time, one day at a time.

# CHAPTER 11

# Inspiration from Other Dads

**A** close friend of mine in college used to speak at length about the relationship he had with his father. The contrast to the relationship I had with mine could not have been greater. My friend not only loved his father tremendously, but he also spoke about how solid and grounded he was as a man and role model. I envied him.

What I came to learn, however, was that his father in his earlier years was a party animal. My friend didn't dwell too long on the stories his father shared about his wild youth, but alcohol played a big role in what sounded like a wild teenage-to-early-twenties lifestyle.

When my friend's father brought his first child into the world, he eliminated his drinking habit entirely. When I asked my friend why his father gave up drinking altogether, he said his dad knew life was about to get serious and he wanted to play an active role. He didn't want to be sidelined with a bad habit that would distance him from his wife and children.

That conversation stood out in my mind. I sensed my friend's father made an honorable and mature decision centered on the importance of fatherhood. One worth emulating.

No one approaches fatherhood with a clean slate; we all have our weaknesses. To elevate your role as a father, if yours was involved in your life, consider his (or your mother's) bad habits. If you harbor similar habits, can you eliminate them from your daily life and provide your son with a better role model?

# CHAPTER 12

# The Anchor Fathers Who Hold You Back

The use of the word "anchor" here refers to how ships use anchors to hold themselves in position, not the talking heads on television. As far as an anchor father, I'm referring to fathers who hold themselves and their kids back from the chance to excel in life due to negative influencers.

You know them, maybe too many of them, depending on your childhood circumstances. These are the guys who have an agenda that doesn't correlate to being a solid role model. It may not be the obvious ones, like the heavy drinkers or the dads who screamed or cursed at their wives. Maybe it was an overbearing dad who thought discipline was best served up through physical means. Maybe you "got out of line," and he made it his mission to ensure you got the message. *His house = his rules.*

These people aren't role models. More likely than not, they are bullies who can't handle the stress or demands that come with being a dad. In some cases, it was better for everyone if they were absent, although some say a father figure, regardless of his shortcomings, is essential.

Well . . . maybe not.

Some dads brought their "baggage" with them and tried to bestow their agendas upon the next generation. Baggage, for those not familiar with the psychological term, represents the ulterior motives people attach to their frame of mind. It could be that parent on the sidelines of a sporting event rooting a little too hard for their son or daughter, or a demanding parent who will accept nothing less than "A" grades, or the parent who attempts to steer their child's interests to suit their own needs (*"I was never known as a great athlete, but my child will be!"*).

Their baggage not only affected their children, but was passed along to them; overbearing dads pass along that playbook to their children. They, in turn, will likely harbor resentments that may arise when they are adults. The adage "the apple doesn't fall far from the tree" is often true.

These dads collectively represent the anchors, the ones holding back their kids.

If this doesn't represent your experience, you have an advantage. When you're setting your foundation of how you will parent—the values you want to espouse—you won't have those anchors weighing you down.

You have the opportunity to write your own playbook and set your foundation. You are not burdened by the principles your father bestowed upon you. You have room to maneuver and adapt; you can choose your own course.

A perfect example of this is racism. No one is ever born with an instinctive need to hate. It represents a learned process, born out of fear, ignorance, or the need for control. If a racist mindset is not present in the house or part of the community, what child is going to lash out at another because their skin is a different color? A child's naiveté may prompt some innocent questions about another person's color, but in the absence of a racist, what would prompt hatred in the mind of a child?

That's the advantage of having an independent mind when it

comes to being a new dad, but not having one as a child. You have control over your own actions, examples, and values.

So what do you need to eliminate from your family dynamic, and what do you want to espouse as a dad? What can you discard from your experience to make yourself a great parent? When it comes to your child, you can literally work with a clean slate if you put your mind to it.

If you agree with this logic so far, the next step will be a piece of cake.

# CHAPTER 13

# Step One: Being There

**B**eing there" means you're likely doing 99 percent more than your father ever did.

It means you show up. Whether it's a diaper change, advising your son about girls, patting his back after a tough sports game, or egging him on to stop slacking off while he's video gaming. You know because you may wonder sometimes if your father had been there, how different would your life be? Would you be a better person, more successful or wealthy, or simply more grounded?

You can dwell on the past, wonder how things could have gone, but you're only wasting time. A therapist would scream at me for saying that, but if you haven't figured it out yet, your presence probably had very little influence on *why* your dad did not play a significant role in your childhood. He likely had another agenda in mind: a habit, a conflict, inner demons that prevented him from stepping up when he should have. You can resent him for it or take the situation for what it is.

Your role as a father is an opportunity to hit the reset button and get it right for your son.

So . . . step one is showing up. Be there for the late-night crying, help your wife when she least expects it, and anchor your schedule and make adjustments to be there for your son day in and day out. You don't have to be the perfect dad, but showing up means you're one step (if not one leap) ahead of what your dad accomplished as a parent.

No greater vindication in life exists than when a man who is raised by a single mother plays a positive role in this own child's life . . . and ideally in a stable two-parent household.

And when you show up, it provides you with the opportunity to acknowledge and overcome your father's shortcomings. He is the one who missed out. You don't need me to tell you that you're a hell of a lot better than that.

# CHAPTER 14

# Full-Time Daddy

Several weekends before I married my wife, we took a long weekend trip with several couples in tow to Las Vegas. One couple had recently married and another got engaged that weekend. It was a terrific trip and half the fun was seeing my wife, who shunned Vegas, surprise herself by having a fantastic time. When you're weeks away from tying the knot (with a great wedding and honeymoon planned and are currently partying with other couples), what's not to love?

We weren't tied down with a mortgage, a house that needed repairs, a crying baby, or massive debt. Fortunately, we didn't leave Vegas with that last element coming back to haunt us.

One night before we went out, we caught an episode of *Jerry Springer*. I'm not a fan of the show, nor will I ever be. In what has become one of his trademarks, we watched an episode where a mother contested the paternity of two would-be/could-be dads. The drama intensified as the episode fanned the flames of tension between the parties. The mother rose from her chair more than once in order to strike a blow at the man seated opposite her, while potential father number two watched from backstage in horror. Then he was brought out to the sound of boos and concerned growls.

It was the usual lousy show that one expects from Jerry Springer. The comic factor for us was that we were in Vegas, which made watching the show all the more a cliché. If you've never visited the city, half the crowd playing slots in the casinos fit the profile of those in Jerry Springer's audience.

The show's final commercial ended and the telltale envelope was passed to Jerry. Its contents held the results of a DNA paternity test that would reveal who the real father was. Springer's audience hushed as he broke the envelope's seal . . .

. . . And all I could say to myself, as a man who grew up without a father, was *How pathetic are these three individuals?* Being identified as a parent in front of an audience of millions was a pathetic spectacle. And once the father was identified, the concern of facing eighteen years of child support flashed across his face when the only thing that should matter is providing a better life to the baby in question.

The show concluded with the mother waving her finger at the DNA-identified father, screaming, "You're going to be a full-time daddy!"

He replied with a sigh and said, "I'll do what I gotta do."

We made jokes about this episode for years; however, in my heart, I thought about how this idiot father, who didn't want to be a dad, was not worthy of being one.

It's a privilege to be a father, to be a committed, involved, and great dad.

Ask yourself: "Am I a full-time daddy?"

# CHAPTER 15

# Locating Where "Stress" Exists

**A** scene in the movie *Saving Private Ryan* opens with American soldiers attempting to get some rest one night. Everyone in the group, except the sniper played by Barry Pepper, is awake and unable to sleep. The others are shocked how their sniper can close his eyes and enjoy what appears to be a restful sleep. Despite the stress and frontline war conditions a few miles away, the sniper snores away like Sleeping Beauty.

We see this in our work lives to a lesser extent. Some people, compared to the majority, possess the means to deal with stress in a calm manner. If someone isn't affected by stress in the same way or level of degree that you are, this can be rather annoying.

The funny thing about "stress" is that it doesn't physically exist. Sources can raise one's stress and cortisol levels in the body, but ultimately, it exists only in one's mind.

Once Junior is born, you will find yourself faced with demanding pressures at work, home, or family situations. Remind yourself that any and all stress-related emotions start and end between your ears. Focus on what is really important—prioritize what is truly worth aggravation and what is not, and drill down to see what you can control about your response.

When speaking to people north of fifty years old, many of them have a better handle on how to manage stress simply because they've lived long enough to know what is and what is not worth attention.

Imagine if we could all do that in our late twenties. Wouldn't that make the next few decades a lot easier?

# CHAPTER 16

# The Concept of Triage: Prioritizing Areas of Stress

During a work seminar I attended years ago, a consultant (tasked with elevating everyone's sales efforts) spoke about how to manage one's time more efficiently through the practice of triage.

Triage, a French term that came into existence during wartime in the 1800s, classified wounded soldiers according to the urgency of their need for care. Those with minor injuries were moved to the side in order to deal with higher-priority patients, meaning those who would quickly die without treatment. Immediate attention was given to those who could be saved, and not those close to death. This process is still in use today.

As parents, we will likely never face such grim war-like conditions, but as we manage work, marriage, kids, and personal goals, the concept of triage can be useful.

For work-related projects, what objectives on your task list require immediate attention? What will have immediate and negative implications if you don't address them right away? What represents a dead-end and time-consuming project that is not a high priority? What can be tabled until tomorrow?

On the home front, if you simultaneously have to feed your child, attend a doctor's appointment, and check email, how can you manage it all and alleviate stress? If the doctor appointment is mission-critical, will a snack keep your child's hunger pains at bay?

How about managing the early evening workout, dinner with your wife, and calling back a relative who will be out of touch and overseas for a month? How can applying the concept of triage help you in this scenario?

Give it a try. If you're feeling a high level of stress, give your tasks the triage treatment and learn how you can better allocate your time.

# CHAPTER 17

# Bad Habits Intensify, Good Habits Multiply

**H**ow's that fourth beer feeling on the twelfth hole? Maybe it's a hit on the hash pipe after a jam session ends, or during the rehearsal itself.

Another guy is leaving the company with the fourth going-away party this month down the street at that beer hall . . . again.

The management meeting is expected to last two hours, as they usually do. A grande-sized coffee with a shot of espresso will keep you sharp. Caffeine keeps you going, as well as Starbucks's bottom line.

You tell your coworker you'll be back in ten minutes. You're heading outside for a smoke.

When you're sleep-deprived, stressed about a sick baby, disgruntled after a hard day of work, or annoyed about a coworker who isn't up to snuff, your "crutch" often becomes a source of escape—a short-term exodus from daily life.

If you have a wife who's called out your shortcomings, you don't need an author like me doing the same. Frankly, it's none of my business. But I can tell you from personal experience, your ability to parent effectively suffers.

Your crutch will inevitably magnify, no matter how many times you tell yourself weed is not addictive. When you have a big presentation in the morning and you're counting on a good night's sleep to prepare, it will be the same night Junior decides to hysterically scream from teething. That fifth cup of coffee will do more harm than good because you can't work that much caffeine out of your system before nightfall.

Things will compound and magnify until you push your responsibilities onto your wife when you're completely exhausted. If that behavior compounds in your relationship, wait until that crutch seems like a necessity to get through the weekend.

I hit that point in the tenth month of my son's life. He was colicky for the first six months and by his half-year mark, a bottle of wine was always present and consumed, in short order. Those two glasses of wine I drank in the evenings grew from a few nights to every night, every week. This affected my sleep and, coupled with some family-related issues and an over ambitious writing project in the early morning hours, I was a mess by my son's first Christmas.

When you get the urge to escape, do one thing: weave an alternative outlet into your life that's manageable. If you work in a city, take a walk down the block and call a friend. Walk away from the TV and pick up that guitar you haven't played in years. At work, zone out momentarily by logging into Amazon to find a good book. Take a pass on that second glass of wine and start layering in good habits. It's remarkably healthier.

The reciprocal scenario . . . which includes texts from your wife about how it's *your* night with the baby monitor and she's *not* giving you another night off . . . kind of sucks.

# CHAPTER 18

# Old Dads versus Young Dads

**D**uring a sales meeting a decade ago, I came to know a coworker who had a unique parenting experience. He was twenty-four when his first child was born. When his second child was born, he was thirty-seven. The thirteen-year gap between his two children was a result of two different marriages, and his two parenting experiences were completely different. He was like many Midwesterners I've met: grounded, honest, hardworking, and polite. And he was more approachable than not when it came to talking about parenting.

I shared with him how excited I was to become a dad, although I was only a year into my marriage. My wife and I planned to have children, but not until after we enjoyed a few vacations overseas. That prompted me to share with him one of my concerns: being an older dad.

He laughed and patted me on the back. He told me I had nothing to worry about and shared a critical advantage older fathers bring to the table. "You will have greater patience."

He admitted that during his first experience as a parent, he had little (if any) patience, which put a great strain on his marriage. Thirteen years later, when his second child was born, he possessed greater wherewithal. He worried less about the little things and took pleasure in seeing his child grow and mature. He was blunt in his overall assessment of himself, but he concluded that he was a better parent the second time around.

This advice came from someone who was in great shape, despite his extra years. He worked out several times a week, and I had no doubt he could out run, out jump, and out bench press me.

That gave me another goal to aim for: I wanted to be able to toss a football around with my son when in my early fifties. Getting in shape *must* be a priority for older fathers. What use is a father to a son if he can't run ten yards for a catch without gasping for air?

If you're a young dad, make patience the virtue you strive to exude every day.

If you're older, make the effort to keep pace with your child's energy level. Increase your physical tolerance so you can keep up with the little tyke.

Besides, being outrun by a two-year-old is just sad.

# CHAPTER 19

# Right Here, Right Now

**W**hatever happened years ago or may happen in future situations is trivial compared to the present day, hour, and minute. If you're too preoccupied worrying about the past or the future, take a moment to refocus. Your child will never be this age again.

Consider the moment when she takes her first step and starts to walk. The next time in her life when she won't be able to do so (without the use of a cane) will be when she's eighty years old. Where did she walk today?

The only real alarm clock in her infant mind is centered on food. She certainly knows how to ring the alarm bell when she's hungry, and she's dependent on you. What did you feed her today?

When it comes to time, a child's perspective on the day is deeper and richer compared to adults. Children retain and remember more than any adult (or teenager for that matter) with whom they share time. What did you do with your child today?

Your daughter isn't worried about money, nor is she concerned about politics, global warming, or a million other things that may or may not happen. She just wants to spend time with you. How much time did you spend with her today?

That meal you share, that walk you take, and that extra moment you enjoy with your daughter today will represent *her* past and *her* memories. There's only one place in time and in the world where you can make all those things happen.

And that's today.

# CHAPTER 20

# When the World is Running Down, You Make the Best of What's Still Around

Recognize the song verse? The Police recorded it decades ago, and in today's electrically charged and divisive political atmosphere, it's fitting.

The song also provides a killer bass riff, which (once inside your head) is hard to forget.

Regardless of your political point of view, our country has never been more on edge. Flip on a news channel, read a newspaper, or open that email news alert and you'll often feel worse after you do so. A sense of unease comes from not knowing what to expect.

This can be concerning when you're a father. Outside of electing different people or demanding the end of gerrymandering (which solidifies congressional districts by political affiliation), you need to take a step back and look at what you can control.

The first step in the process can be as easy as deciding what TV channels to broadcast in your house. If you find the news upsetting, discuss with your wife when news should and should not be consumed. You may think this is the equivalent of sticking your head in the sand like an ostrich, but you can choose to keep the news to a minimum during family time.

The second step is to control your social media news feed. Did you get caught up on your side of the political fence during the recent election? Did you "like" one too many pages affiliated with politics? "Unfollow" them and reduce your exposure to news sources that have concerned you in the past. You can visit them in the future, but if you remain a fan and continue to like those pages, they will keep reappearing on Facebook, Twitter, etc.

The third step is about what you can control on a more personal, fulfilling level. Look for local volunteer projects or organizations that make a positive impact on the people in your community. Exercise and get healthy, which not only represents a great stress reliever, but it's a life extender too. Try to find outlets where your child can garner a wider and more diverse perspective on the world that will empower them with a broader understanding of and respect for different points of view.

Lastly, be the best father you can be. It may seem trivial in light of so many national challenges, but the decisions you make today can, at the very least, inspire your son to do something positive with his life. Multiply that times millions of caring mothers and fathers and the world may turn out to be a better place for your child, and for your grandkids as well.

# CHAPTER 21

# Give Yourself Some Credit

**W**hether it is six months after becoming a father or two years, you have to pause and take note of what you've accomplished.

Your son or daughter is healthy, playing with the nanny, or waking up at his grandmother's house in the afternoon. You have food in the fridge, a hundred bucks in your wallet, and perhaps your car loan is paid off. The bank or landlord has not evicted you, your front lawn is not the disaster it once was, and you got halfway through the honey-do list last month. (For the record, there is no end to that to-do list! It's like an infinite scroll that unfolds endlessly before you until your untimely death.)

But you've got the basics covered—all of them. Most importantly, it feels as if you've spent more time with your son or daughter over the past few months or years compared to all the time you had with your dad. That's something to feel great about, so treat yourself right. And right now.

Put the kid to sleep, grab a Red Bull so you remain conscious in the movie theatre, and catch the latest installment of Star Wars or a Quentin Tarantino flick, if that's your thing. Go on Amazon.com and buy that watch you've had your eye on for months (if not years). Get a massage or book an afternoon of golf with your best friends.

Live a little, dude. Feel good about where you are. Then get back to the business of being a responsible father.

PART 2

# Your Wife

# CHAPTER 22

# Section Preview: Your Wife

If you have never watched the movie *When Harry Met Sally*, it is one of the better movies ever produced about couples and relationships. Regardless of the era in which the movie was made, it still punctuates the true value of marriage to me.

The film features a series of vignettes with real-life couples talking about their marriage. These couples have been married for decades . . . *decades*! The husbands and wives not only express love for one another, they also espouse an endearing commitment that has stayed true for many years. These men and women either rediscovered their love later in life or their marriage lasted fifty-plus years. Many of the husbands featured were World War Two veterans who were lucky enough to make it home alive.

Each couple expresses a deep commitment to one another. They were all at the tail end of life when the movie was filmed, and I'd be surprised if any of them are still alive. But the most beautiful element about their relationships was they still, after so many years, had each other.

Their physical appearance didn't matter, nor their financial status or place of residence. They had someone by their side through good times and bad, and now they enjoyed their golden years together. I can't imagine what it was like when one partner passed away and the surviving spouse was left alone; surely they were grief stricken.

Likewise, I truly can't picture my life without my wife by my side. I hope you feel the same. I love the sound of her laughter, her sense of humor, and witnessing the love she expresses to me and our son, Connor. Sometimes I imagine the two of us being filmed in our later years like the couples in *When Harry Met Sally*. Where we will be? Where will we have traveled to and what memories will we have shared? I think about the future and how we will share important holidays with my son, his future wife, and our grandchildren. These kinds of hopes and dreams motivate me as a father and a husband.

You may share other hopes and dreams, and perhaps different qualities about your wife resonate in a special way with you. That's what makes your marriage special. Now that you are parents, treat her as an equal partner in every respect. No one will ever discredit you for trying to be a great husband and father, and doing so will provide the means to strengthen the family bonds you share with your loved ones.

You can set a new and stronger foundation, one that transcends what your parents were able to provide.

# CHAPTER 23

# Your Marriage Is Your Institution

**Y**ou've chosen a partner—someone you trust, love, and hopefully consider your best friend. This is your compatriot in good times and bad. Someone to lean on, and the most trusted person in your life.

Your wife and you represent an institution. That, more than anything else, is your number one priority.

Together, you will decide how to raise your kids and what values to pass on to them. The decisions you make will hopefully give your child a better life. It's a beautiful thing, but it will not always be easy.

If you come from a divorced household, or one where your father was a negative influence, you may not have experienced two parents acting as a team. Yet the best parenting represents a team effort, and you and your wife—*both* of you—must make sound decisions together.

Equally important is committing to a decision process that keeps outside influences in check. No matter what other family members may think, you and your wife have the final say on everything that relates to your child.

You may have goals in mind of how you want to parent together, but parents who come from divorced homes inevitably have a skewed perception of the role each parent plays.

The key is *communication*. Share the goals or concerns you have with your spouse; find the kinks and work your way through them together. Manage challenges jointly and in advance before they boil over, even if they are long-standing fears you or your spouse may hold. If you don't, issues will simmer and eventually spill over in a state of anger, and usually at the worst time.

It's better to let the steam out of the pot in slow doses. You married your spouse for a number of great reasons, so keep that bond rock solid when things get rough. And when things get heated, remember . . . she's your partner for life. If you parent as a true team, your child has a better chance of not going through what you did as a child. Unlike the single mom who either exclusively or predominantly raised you, you now *have* someone—a partner with whom to share all the experiences of parenting.

Your marriage, no matter the challenges you face or the obstacles you encounter, is worth preserving. And in doing so, you will create a stronger family structure than what you may have experienced as a child. Do it together—as a team.

## CHAPTER 24
# Your Parents' Divorce, Translated

I'm willing to bet that a large percentage of the income psychologists and therapists derive from their job relates to divorce. Not the act itself, or the effort to save a marriage, but from dealing with the long-term aftermath of divorce . . . especially on the children.

If you're a child of divorced parents, you can watch the scene in *Good Will Hunting* when Robin Williams repeatedly tells Matt Damon it's not his fault perhaps a hundred times, and you may relate to it in a hundred different ways. That's the core message the psychologist community tries to instill— that divorce is not the fault of the child—and they make a great living doing so. I'm not taking a jab at their profession, but the tangled mess that results from divorce lasts—on some level—one's entire life.

Maybe you can mentally put that part of your childhood in a box, write off the loss of your parents' union, and move forward. One area, however, must be addressed, and it begins and ends with the person lying beside you in bed at night— your spouse. (If there's someone else in your bed with you on a routine basis, you have other issues, my friend.)

The best thing you can do for yourself is to focus on your marriage and the relationship and bond you have with your wife. What can you improve upon? Perhaps think about what went wrong between your parents; if you can identify certain patterns of behavior that marked their marriage and relationship, and then see those same patterns emerge between you and your wife, what are the odds your kid will suffer from divorce just as you did as a child?

According to Nicholas Wolfinger's *Understanding the Divorce Cycle*,[1] the likelihood of a couple divorcing when one spouse was raised by divorced parents is 40 percent higher compared to individuals raised by parents who remained married. If both spouses were raised in a divorced household, the likelihood of divorce increases by 200 percent! That's a hard fact to swallow, but now that you are aware of this, you're ahead of the curve. By addressing your shortcomings and/or your wife's, you're giving your child a huge advantage. The greater a couple's awareness, communication, and teamwork, the greater the chance your kids won't have to experience their parents getting divorced.

If you want to place the regrets you have about your parents' divorce in a box and stash it away, no one will blame you. Just remember what that figurative "box" looks like. Note the packaging, size, and weight. If your marriage starts to look anything like it—in form or substance—start communicating more with your wife; it will help keep the skeletons at bay.

---

1    Wolfinger, Nicholas H. *Understanding the Divorce Cycle: The Children of Divorce in their Own Marriages.* Cambridge University Press, 2005.

# CHAPTER 25

# Your Parents' Marriage versus Your Marriage: The Milestone Year

If your parents divorced before you graduated high school, I'd like to give you something to consider.

Go back and figure out how many years they were married. It doesn't have to be exact, perhaps the length of time between marriage and separation, or when the final divorce papers were signed. Your heart will tell you what timespan is most relevant to this exercise.

Let's say their marriage lasted ten years in total. They had you one year after they married. When you turned seven, according to one or both of them, things started getting difficult. You recall the moment when you were nine and they sat you down for a chat that resulted in an extremely grown-up conversation, one that left you more confused than before it happened. For years, you may have blamed yourself for your parents' divorce.

Flash forward to the present. Your baby is upstairs sleeping, or perhaps you're commuting home to your pregnant wife. How many years have you been married? Now subtract that number from the total number of years your parents were married.

How long do you have left to go until your marriage surpasses your parents' marriage? Six years? Maybe ten? On which of your wedding anniversaries will your marriage have outlasted your parents'?

From a divorced child's perspective, doesn't that represent an absolutely fantastic reason to celebrate? Think about it: Individuals from divorced homes are at a higher risk of getting divorced themselves. You and your spouse are on your way to a long future together. Consider how that will benefit your children.

If you see the logic in this, then make reaching this particular milestone a special event. Do something outrageous with your wife (and her alone). Go to Paris for a long weekend. Splurge on diamond earrings. Take a trip to Napa, in Northern California's romantic wine country. Surprise her and tell her why your twelfth anniversary, for example, is more meaningful to you than she could ever comprehend.

You will both have a great reason to celebrate because you have each other and your marriage has endured.

# CHAPTER 26
# The Hard Questions

If you zig every time your wife zags, or your solution to an issue contrasts with your spouse's, it's time to hit the reset button.

If you're bickering about the color of your child's room, or if it relates to common, everyday work-related stress, you're probably doing okay. If, however, you have fundamental problems that continue to arise, then it's time to go back to square one before you take the next step—therapy.

One example where long-term spousal disagreements may pop up is when relatives "pop in" unexpectedly. If your mom or mother-in-law lives close and stops by, and it represents a source of tension between you and your spouse, you need to discuss it. This touches on how you and your wife represent an independent institution as parents.

I note this because if you believe in the concept of family and want to provide your child with a better upbringing and more stable household than you experienced, I have a suggestion.

When my wife and I were engaged, a relative gave me a copy of a book called *The Hard Questions: 100 Questions to Ask Before You Say I Do* by Susan Piver. On some level, it was awkward to be given the book, but my wife and I read it several months after I proposed to her. It requests that you read it together, and one spouse asks the other person half the questions, and vice versa for the second half. It covers the topic of children, of course, and lots of other important subjects, such as how you will manage families, religion, money, etc.

At points the book is repetitive, but getting your "house" in order before or shortly after your daughter enters the world is critical. Perhaps you planned to work out some issues in the future and your wife became pregnant earlier than expected. Now issues are arising that you didn't expect and there seems to be no simple way to end the stress.

Start with Susan Piver's book and work through its hard questions over several nights. Find out where the pain points exist, communicate with each other, and try to work through them. Come to an agreement that—even if it doesn't make you completely satisfied—you can live with.

Face the challenges hampering your marriage and you'll have a more stable family foundation.

And if that doesn't work, don't give up on your marriage; instead, find a recommended therapist. The couple that works to preserve their marriage represents two people trying to give their child a better life.

That makes the process worthwhile, don't you think?

# CHAPTER 27
# Land Mines

**Y**ou've had a tough week. Maybe the boss was riding you about a project coming up on a deadline, or the commute was more brutal than usual. Perhaps it's a new job and you're trying to get a grasp of the politics in play.

If your wife is a stay-at-home mom and your child is sick, colicky, or simply pushing the limits a grown human being can endure, trust your wife had a tougher week than you. It's no debate: Your rough week does not compare to what she's put up with. You likely experienced this yourself already, but commuting, an overbearing boss, and work responsibilities can dim one's short-term memories.

Your wife doesn't have the luxury of getting the same break from parenting you do. During the week, her days are solely focused on taking care of an infant without the day-to-day camaraderie or interaction you enjoy with adults while in the office. Alternatively, if she is a working parent, she's also weighed down by work-related stress, like yourself.

You will at some point walk in the door, open your mouth, and say or do something out of line, and the slightest infraction will set your wife off in a rampage. She will overreact and it will be obvious that the punishment does not fit the crime.

You might either walk away and sleep on the couch, cursing yourself for marrying a grade-A b*tch, or you will put on the gloves and fight back twice as hard. Either option delivers the same result where you dig a deeper hole for both of you.

Sometimes you simply must give her some space, absorb the blows, and take it for what it is—a mom who lost her temper. She's letting off steam and it is directed at you, the only other adult in the house.

Rather than fight back, defuse the situation; tell her how much you love her, and tell her you're there for her. Straighten up the toys, do a load of laundry, and take the high road. At some point, she's going to look back at the incident and realize she was way out of line, and your actions *after* the land mine went off represent your dedication as a father and a husband.

And a few hours later, when you share a laugh about it, make sure you thank her as sarcastically as possible for planting all those land mines around the front door. And demand make-up sex. Every . . . single . . . time.

## CHAPTER 28

# When Your Wife Really Pisses You Off

This chapter is oriented more around your marriage than your role as a father, but bear with me. The end goal is the same: not getting into a screaming match in front of your son or daughter.

My mother got her master's degree in psychology later in life and shared with me many concepts, lessons, and tools she learned. One principle especially relevant to this chapter is called "empathetic conflict resolution."

Here's the situation: There is a major disturbance in the force. Yoda himself can feel the tremors reverberating in your head about an issue you have with your wife. I'm not talking about anything extreme like adultery, but, nevertheless, your wife has really pissed you off. Perhaps it was a transgression at a social gathering, or she made an off-hand remark that was way out of line. She might have accused you of making a mistake repeatedly when it's not the case. Either way, the voice inside your head is saying *She is WAY out of line!*

The worst-case scenario is that you get so mad you end up screaming at her. This, in turn, requires you to apologize, despite the fact that she also owes *you* an apology.

But the empathetic conflict resolution approach takes a different path. First, identify your wife's behavior; second, explain how it affects you and makes you feel.

To give you a better idea of how this concept works in a real-life situation, here are two examples:

- "Honey, when I have to shovel the driveway after work and you accuse me of not helping out enough afterwards, it really upsets me. I'm trying to tackle something that's kind of urgent, and it wears me out, so I'd like to know how I'm letting you down."

- "When you tell me my weekly tennis game is taking time away from the family, it makes me feel horrible because I realize that I'm getting exercise, but you haven't pursued any of your own hobbies. What can I do to give you the free time you need?"

You may think these responses sound feminine in nature, but does either example give your spouse an opening to attack you? No. Rather, you have expressed how you feel, while also giving a dose of empathy.

Try this approach when you're really frustrated. Don't start off with "We have to talk," or "We need to sit down and hash this out." Women can smell that stink miles away, and they will have their guard up the minute you open your mouth.

# CHAPTER 29

# A Heavy Subject

The second after you tell your wife it's time to lose the baby weight, the result will be the longest night, weekend, and possibly month you will endure as a husband.

Try a better approach. Both you and your wife owe it to yourselves to take care of your health and well-being. Your ability to be physically active with your daughter will result in you being a better father because you'll be able to participate athletically. The same is true for your wife.

The time leading up to fatherhood and the first year or two of your daughter's life will not provide much time for you or your spouse to exercise. So team up with your wife to tackle the challenge together. Ask her if she wants to start eating healthier with you and suggest long walks with the stroller to get started. Trim back on late-night snacking, set some goals, and drop weight *together*.

It makes everything easier. You can watch out for one another when shopping for food or learning how to cook healthier recipes. Strengthen your endurance and buy a jogging stroller or go for long hikes with a Baby Bjorn and enjoy some scenery.

Taking the journey with your spouse will eliminate the post-birth stress and insecurity she is likely experiencing. She's probably never carried around so much extra weight in her entire life.

Besides, if your mother-in-law hears about how you asked her daughter (i.e., your wife) to drop the baby weight, the guilt trip she'll inflict upon you will last for decades.

# CHAPTER 30
# There Is Nothing Worse . . .

. . . you can do as a father than cheat on your wife and act on a sexual impulse today that will require you to apologize to your child for the rest of your life.

# CHAPTER 31
# Own Up to It

You woke up on the wrong side of the bed, had a bad commute, and the afternoon meeting with your boss could have gone a lot better. To top it off, the evening commute was even worse than the morning.

Then you opened the front door and it only took the slightest infraction to set off your short fuse. Your voice rose in volume and, soon enough, something that bothered you last week got thrown into the discussion. After exchanging verbal jabs, you stormed off, found a distant room, and slammed the door shut.

Then you heard the baby cry—perhaps your son was either getting changed or fed—but you weren't ready to face or deal with your better half again.

After a fight, consider what your mindset was before angry words were exchanged. Put the content of what was said aside and consider the context of your circumstances. Even if you are 100 percent sure the issue at hand was something you disagreed with, own up to your short fuse and apologize.

The example you set and owning up to your shortcomings will set the foundation for how your child faces a similar circumstance in their own life. Regardless of their age and what they will remember, the earlier you start figuring out how to resolve conflicts, the better.

If the issue needs to be addressed, table it until Junior is bathed and asleep and you've done your share of the work as a father. Kissing your kid good night when you're holding your wife's hand puts everything into perspective.

# CHAPTER 32

# Stating the Obvious— Good Times

On my wedding day, my grandmother gave me the single best piece of advice I ever received when it came to marriage. I prompted her to share it with me, and given how my parents' marriage ended, I thought it was wise to do so. Her marriage lasted well over thirty years before my grandfather's death. My parents split before I was six.

Here's what she told me: "You're going to have good times; you're going to have bad times. Remember the good times."

That was it. Short, sweet, and (as is often the case when it comes to advice) the simpler, the better.

When you're in the throes of parenting in the first year, there's an adjustment phase. Couples clash. It's inevitable when frustrations, lack of sleep, and unexpected tensions come to the surface.

When times are going well, state the obvious—tell your wife how much you enjoyed spending time with her and your child. Highlight what went well, pay attention to the good times, and voice them all to your wife. It helps to provide perspective, and talking about the good times goes a lot further than rehashing what didn't go so well.

Every couple during that first year of a child's life goes through rough times. Remember the good times.

# CHAPTER 33

# The Good Weekend

It's Sunday night, 10:30 p.m. You turn off the nightstand light, lean back, and rest your head on the pillow. You're exhausted after a busy weekend, which happens more often now given you're a full-time dad. Your wife is beside you, tooling around on her iPad and just zoning out.

You realize that for the first time in what seems like an eternity, your family just had a fantastic weekend. Less crying occurred for reasons you can't fully explain, the bickering or nagging was minimal, and you and your wife shared some laughs and got a chance to enjoy each other's company. You second-guess yourself when you try to remember a weekend that went so well, but you can't refute it.

In the first six months, or even during the first full year after your child is born, good weekends happen less frequently compared to the newlywed years. In-laws show up unexpectedly, you or your wife flakes out on an important holiday or birthday, or you accuse each other of letting the other down when it came to responsibilities.

It can be a challenging time, but why do I state the obvious? Let me explain.

When you have a great family weekend, and on that Sunday night when you go to bed, turn to your wife and tell her you had a great weekend with her and you love her. She'll appreciate the fact. But if she shrugs her shoulders, nudge her and ask what could have gone better? Unless you're completely blind to your shortcomings, you'll know if the weekend was a good one for your family.

And if she *still* pushes back, tell her you're offended and require make-up sex for her short-sightedness. Do it right then . . . and try to keep your mind preoccupied with baseball or something, because you're probably not the sex machine you were before the baby came along.

# CHAPTER 34

# When It's Time to Call in the Referee

They are loved and hated, those NFL officials who don zebra costumes. Although they are never 100 percent accurate, for the most part they make the right call. And thankfully, for everyone, the refs can check their calls via instant replays. When a coach tosses a red flag from the sidelines, there's a better-than-average chance a bad call will be reversed.

If you watch NFL games, you know how this drama plays out. The penalty occurs and the coach delays a decision to challenge the call, but he's listening intently on his headphones while the crowd screams for justice. The visiting team has perpetrated a vile penalty! The opposition lines up on offense, hurrying to formation, but seconds before a play is called, the red flag is dropped on the field of play. Rousing applause follows.

A time comes in everyone's marriage when each spouse, feeling wronged by their partner, wants to toss the red flag. If things fester or the conflict goes unresolved, one bad day can turn into a bad week, then possibly become a month of lingering conflict and friction. I'm not referring to day-to-day bickering; rather, this relates to more serious issues, like uprooting the family for a new job, in-laws that disrupt your nuclear family, or different approaches to parenting.

If you start to feel like your spouse is a constant adversary, you have to consider tossing the red flag. When there's a child involved (or one on the way), you should not hesitate for one second: Toss the red flag and call in the ref.

The ref, in this analogy, represents a therapist or family counselor. If you are one of the millions of men who grew up with a single parent, you should feel no shame or guilt for doing everything you can to preserve your marriage. A third party can provide perspective about your decision-making process, and they will undoubtedly look back at you and your wife's family histories (in essence, instant replays of them). Therapists can help you make connections between present-day conflicts and your pasts. A good therapist can reveal where each partner's blind spots are in a manner that doesn't put either spouse in a corner. This process often reveals more truth than not, and can help you set new ground rules so you can move forward together.

Every part of one's parenting life—the costs, the labor, the agreements necessary to educate a child, disciplining, and the overall time commitment—is doubled in terms of sweat and tears when a couple divorces. A child shuttled back and forth from one parent's home to another is proof alone . . . You may have experienced this yourself.

You and your wife both owe your son the effort of saving the relationship that led to his birth in the first place by working with a therapist. Then, even if your efforts fail, you will be able to tell your son you did everything you could to keep the family intact. Almost every child of divorce blames themselves for their parents' break up at some point. Going to therapy proves you did everything you could to preserve your marriage.

If you do separate and divorce, you've got an important lesson to pass on to your boy: Marriage is an institution worth fighting for, and you and your spouse made every effort to save it. That experience may provide the foundation your child needs when he marries and faces similar circumstances.

# CHAPTER 35

# The "Man" of the House

Even if you have some preconceived notion relating to the 1950s type of dad (the one who possesses unquestionable authority and represents the exclusive breadwinner), as a modern dad you're probably not kicking off your shoes the moment you walk in the door and asking when dinner will be ready. Rather, you are likely helping your wife get your daughter ready for bed, doing some cooking, or straightening up around the house.

So as the "man of the house," you will need downtime in the evening, perhaps even more than that 1950s stereotype of a father.

Set a time (a schedule of sorts for yourself) for every night of the week. At a certain hour, it's time to settle down so you can relax. It's best spent with your spouse, who deserves an equal (if not greater, if she is a stay-at-home mom) amount of relaxation time. Of course, the first choice to end the day when you're relaxing is sex, but you already know that. But sex does not require scheduling (per se) because, first, that's not very romantic. And second, your better half is likely not keen on scheduling that element of her life.

The main goal is setting downtime for yourself *before* you go to bed. If the daily routine doesn't feel like it ends entirely until you go to bed, this will lead to parental insanity. You and your wife need a break after a full day, and agreeing on a time when you will set aside the routine and simply relax will keep you both sane.

What is the reciprocal scenario that leads to parental insanity? Not having sex.

Knock boots, not heads.

# CHAPTER 36

# If You're Always Being Told What to Do, Congratulations— You've Been Emasculated

The title of this chapter may come across as rather terse, but it happens. Men come home from work and their wives have (what they believe to be) everything worked out and decided.

In some cases when it comes to feeding schedules, nap times, or daily patterns, it's completely acceptable. In the case of two working parents, both parents may be so overwhelmed with daycare drop-offs and pick-ups that the father succumbs to his wife's decisions simply because it's less of a hassle.

For certain decisions, however, a conversation between you and your spouse about potential consequences or results may be required. The topic could be any number of things, but when it comes to child development, stay engaged and ask questions if you want to ensure your role as an active parent. It's not worth causing a ruckus over trivial matters, but more important decisions will linger beyond your child turning two.

If your wife is a stay-at-home mother who is nursing your child, she may feel entitled to make decisions without your consent, particularly if she's the caregiver 24/7 due to breastfeeding; however, you brought this child into the world as well, and you should address anything that concerns you.

Simply say, "Let's talk about that before we jump in head first," and make your point. If you let your wife call all the shots, the hill gets steeper as time goes on if your goal is to parent on an equal level.

# CHAPTER 37

# Over-Servicing: Your Wife's Honey-Do List

Since the dawn of humanity, an ever-present tension has existed between husbands and wives. Men use a term to identify husbands who seem to be under their wife's finger: pussy-whipped.

This phrase is often used during the girlfriend/boyfriend relationship status, but less so once a man steps into the role of fatherhood. An element of responsibility shelters a person once he is a father. Friends who continue to mock a man after he becomes a father tend to make fools out of themselves.

But it begs the question: How often are you kowtowing to your wife? Did you lose your spine when you tied the knot? Are you finding your weekends jam-packed from taking care of the unending honey do list?

Look at that list and break it down into two categories: 1) What requests are important to her, and 2) What requests are important to the family? If you find something on the list that's not a high priority for anyone other than your wife, perhaps it's time to talk about it.

For anything else, whether it's keeping the bathroom extra clean, throwing out diaper bags, or taking extra care of the pet, then "over-service" her on some of those requests. The less important ones are just that. Are you really "whipped" if you go the extra mile to help her, or are you being a good partner and husband? More importantly, is your kid happier and healthier given what you're providing?

Being the man of the house is knowing how to prioritize and, more importantly, doing it in a diplomatic manner.

# CHAPTER 38

# Dating Your Wife

Through the chaos of waking up for early feedings and keeping on top of work and routines, a critical element that binds husbands and wives together is sometimes lost.

That of course . . . is romance! Through the haze of weariness and taking on greater responsibilities that come with fatherhood, it's important to remember what led to having kids in the first place. I'm not speaking about epic sex romps on multiple nights of the week. (Hopefully that is a given in your relationship.) But you've got to treat your woman right—before, during, and after you're married.

Go the extra mile and treat her to a great meal and a movie. Spend quality time together without checking your phone every five minutes for updates from the babysitter. You owe it to your spouse to ensure she knows how much you enjoy spending time with her. It sounds like a no-brainer, but without even knowing it, you may go one, two, or even three months without spending some quality time with your better half.

You may even want to schedule something in your calendar, like a monthly reminder. There's no shame in that. Get it on the books and take her to her favorite restaurant.

You're likely not going to take your eye off what matters (your child's health, progress at work, helping around the house when you can, etc.). If you discover that time and daily events have dimmed the spark of romance between you and your wife, douse those embers with a can of lighter fluid.

Science has also proven that romantic evenings result in more sex. Get going with romance and you'll probably get lucky.

# CHAPTER 39
# The Nursing Mother

It's impossible for a father to care for a child on equal terms with a mother who's nursing her infant.

Even if your wife pumps breast milk and you have a freezer stuffed with plastic bottles, you physically do not possess the means to provide the same level of care. Try as you might to espouse equality and responsibility, the nursing mother trumps all when it comes to the act of giving everything she has for your daughter.

So what can you do to elevate your role as the father? Give your wife a block of time (every week) she can have to herself without any questions or headaches. Start a ritual with your daughter, like breakfast at a friendly diner followed by a visit to the playground, or take over bathing duties and tuck your girl into bed after reading her a book. Give your wife a full day once a month to hang out with friends, visit a relative, or do whatever else she wants.

She more than likely deserves it. And if the idea comes from you, you'll not only be a champion for suggesting it, but every time you provide her that freedom, she'll feel grateful.

That's not only being a good parent, it's also being a good husband.

# CHAPTER 40

# A Second Child on Your Terms

**W**hen you have one baby and he's healthy and happy, the inevitable question gets asked: "Are you planning to have more kids?"

When your child is misbehaving, how many times are you asked this same question? It's kind of ironic that parents only field this question when Junior is behaving like a saint. No one traveling with you on an airplane will ask that question if your daughter is screaming non-stop for an hour.

A ton of reasons exist why other parents inquire about this, and it's become somewhat of a ritual. Perhaps other parents hold a high opinion of you as a father and want to see you have more kids. It could also be from envy. Or maybe they are thinking about having another child and subconsciously bounce the idea off you to question their own family plans.

Sometimes a pregnancy test one way or the other decides the future of one's family. But for you and your wife, you have to remove the societal pressure to have another child because that decision is best left for just the two of you.

Ask yourself (and your wife) these two simple questions when it comes to having more kids:

1. Do you want to have a second child to serve his/her needs or your own?
2. Can you give everything you are already giving to child number one to child number two?

The two questions go hand-in-hand because if you can't provide everything to child number two, then perhaps you're serving your own needs first. If you are already not giving child number one everything she needs to excel, how are you going to manage to do that (and more) if a second child is in the picture?

Having another child is a gift in itself and should never be taken for granted. But if you are fertile, young, and want a second child, make sure it's on you and your wife's terms—exclusively.

# PART 3

## Your Child

# CHAPTER 41

# Section Preview: Your Child

**D**oes it get any better?

Bringing a newborn home represents the greatest joy and life-altering moment a couple will ever share. It also represents the biggest "life balancer." If you've endured five, ten, or twenty years in the workforce, the thrill of coming home from a hard day and having your barely-able-to-walk child come running toward you is a moment of pure love.

I'm getting ahead of myself, given this book is drafted for expecting fathers and those with infants in the house. That brings me to my first point.

*It gets easier.*

As you struggle from lack of sleep, friction with a nursing wife, or ever-present bills, I can guarantee you it gets easier with time. The first two years go by in a blur and you'll go through a few developmental stages, but rest assured that each year gets easier than the last. The rewards are enormous—you will literally watch your child evolve and grow, and before you know it, you're sharing conversations with him or her.

Children absorb everything and represent a reflection of you and your wife in the early years. This leads to my second point.

*Your child's perception of the world provides you a fresh perspective on your world.*

It's a new take on everything. When was the last time you had the opportunity to experience that? To enjoy it, there is only one requirement: your involvement. You will likely never have the chance to do this again until you're a grandparent, but even at that stage, you won't be as involved compared to being a father on the frontlines of parenthood.

Here's one last thing to keep in mind: *There's no pause button in life.*

Once children go through one stage, they are on to the next. Be present for it all, and don't risk missing any part. Soak it in and reward your child with your company and guidance. Speaking from experience, if you missed having a father present during childhood, sharing your child's experience at every stage of development offers comfort and some level of healing. For fathers who come from divorced homes, knowing how much better you are as a dad compared to your own represents redemption on some level.

# CHAPTER 42

# Stage 1: The First Four Months = Teamwork

**H**undreds, if not thousands, of books have been published on baby care. Many of them are exceptional, and the bestsellers are just that for a reason—babies do not come with instructional manuals.

If you are an expecting father, this chapter and the following two briefly suggest one immediate goal to focus on at different stages during the first year of your child's life.

Stage 1 represents the first four months of your child's life. **Keep your focus on teamwork** and it will help you get to the next stage.

You and your wife now have the most important job you will ever do. Working with one another as parents in the first four months trumps all other priorities. Communication is critical, and if you need to figure out who's going to manage household chores (laundry, food shopping, etc.), write it down and stick to it. It may seem silly to designate one of you to manage certain tasks, but it will keep your house in order. If you can designate bills to be paid automatically, do so and it will free up time to do other things.

Stage 1 can be all-consuming, and the lack of sleep and personal time may prompt fights over trivial matters. That's not what good teammates do, so figure out a plan.

# CHAPTER 43

# Stage 2: Growth and Adjustment (4–9 months old)

During Stage 2, you'll see your daughter smile for the first time. She'll start to express her personality, involve herself with more toys, and begin to crawl. A hint of independence will appear. Her reactions and physical capabilities will further develop.

During this stage, **take the time to encourage her**. Help her with her words and stay involved as much as you can. It's an exciting time during her development, and the responsiveness you'll witness only begets greater activity.

During this stage, you will see your efforts—which may seem redundant and tedious at times—pay off if you encourage your daughter along the way. You also may spot a pattern of behavior that gives you a reason to pause. You may find she doesn't always respond when she hears your voice; perhaps her hearing is better in one ear compared to the other. You might notice she is not interacting with toys; her sight may not be 20/20. Staying close and attuned to your daughter's behavior and needs may reveal issues that you can address early in her development.

This is also the last time of her life in which she won't be mobile. Crawling can start as early as four months, and walking is not far thereafter.

With two parents committed to her development, your daughter will accelerate her language skills as well.

## CHAPTER 44
# Stage 3: Safety (9–16 months old)

**W**hen Stage 3 begins, it won't be long until your son wanders into another room. Pretty soon, wandering leads to full-on sprints into other parts of the house.

Now is the time to **babyproof your house** from top to bottom. Get the baby gates up, check to make sure valuable items or choking hazards are kept out of reach, kneel down to get an eye-level view of what your son may or may not run into head-first, get plastic plugs for the electrical sockets, and check to make sure there are no items he can pull on and injure himself.

Go from one room to the next and spend quality time in each place to ensure you're not missing something you may have over-looked. Are there any items your son could swallow (pet toys, for example)? Are the cabinets where you keep cleaning products childproofed?

You'll be surprised what a relief it is to address your son's safety in advance of him walking. Now the only thing you have to worry about is his whereabouts when he begins to sprint around. You've got some time before you're running after him . . . but not much.

So get ahead (and stay ahead) of any safety concerns. It will put you and your wife's minds at ease.

And your child reaching his first birthday is worthy of a big celebratory party—not only for him, but also for you and your wife.

# CHAPTER 45
# Your Kid's Childhood Is a Treasure

**Y**ou're human, so you've likely reflected on your younger days. As you get older, you may recall your childhood even more frequently, both the highs and the lows. Reminiscing is both a blessing and a curse; it can either warm your soul or sour your mood.

For those of us who grew up in divorced homes, childhood memories contrast hugely. The distance between fantastic memories and ugly ones is greater compared to the rest of the population. You only need to read Bruce Springsteen's autobiography to get a feel for what I'm talking about. But in one particular chapter, he associates childhood as a type of treasure, and it truly can be.

The treasure Springsteen writes about is oriented around good times, and, reciprocally, some influences in his life dimmed the light of his childhood.

Who had the most negative effect on Springsteen's childhood? His father.

Maybe this relates to you, but even if it doesn't, isn't it your job to try to provide your daughter with a treasure chest filled with warm childhood memories? Is there anything you can do to insulate her from a bad habit or instinct? Perhaps you have a temper, or you and your spouse argue in front of your daughter. These kinds of examples do not reflect your value as a father overall, but they may leave an indelible impression on the next generation.

If you can course correct one negative pattern of behavior, you'll give your daughter a slightly bigger treasure chest of positive memories to reflect on later in life.

## CHAPTER 46
# When You Have Zero Patience

**A**s you pass from one stage to the next—from endless nights, to spit up on your work clothes, to your daughter sprinting toward the fireplace—you will eventually break down and hit a wall.

The wall represents the last of your patience. Your brain will scream for the crying in the backseat to end, or you would die for just four consecutive hours of sleep. You're at your wit's end, and no amount of coffee can alleviate the weariness of being actively involved in your child's life.

Pat yourself on the back at these crazy-making moments because you're doing more than your father likely ever did during his life when it came to raising kids. That's your inner salvation: You are not a part-time parent. You are in the trenches.

This is easy to say in hindsight, but it is the point. However challenging things are at this moment, they will be gone in less time than you think as your child enters a new stage of life.

Let the past remain behind you and push forward. The present is where you need to be. If your daughter is up late with a bad cold, she will recover. If you cannot take a bite when your family is out to dinner without your child spitting up, take a doggy bag and enjoy it when she's down for the night. The more you can manage your temper when the moment is tense, the better man and father you will be for it.

Your wife and your family will take notice. As trivial as it may sound, you are rising to the occasion and dealing with it like a great dad.

Because if you do—more than likely—you are one.

# CHAPTER 47

# Struggles and Success

In Mark Manson's book *The Subtle Art of Not Giving a F\*ck*, he sums up the secret of success in one phrase:

"Our struggles determine our success."

When you're at your wit's end—tired, frustrated, short-fused, and up again for the third time in the middle the night—remember . . . If you want to be a successful parent, the struggles you endure reflect your commitment. Could you be a father, a good one, without having to endure those struggles?

If you can do it with a level head and exude grace under pressure, you're on your way to being a great dad.

Aim high.

# CHAPTER 48
# Parenting Is a Privilege

**W**hether you are in the trenches with a colicky baby, months away from welcoming your daughter into the world, or hearing the screams of your son six times throughout the night, here's some relevant wisdom:

"You'll have good times, you'll have bad times. Remember the good times."

This was the advice given to me by my ninety-year-old grandmother on the day of my wedding, and it applies to parenting as well. If you are dragging your feet as you walk into the door at work or ready to pull your hair out with a screaming baby in the backseat of the car, keep in mind that parenting is, and should be considered, a privilege.

If you want to be one of those dads who whine and moan about the trials and tribulations of raising a child, bear in mind what others think when you share your complaints. You may know people who cannot biologically have children or are trying to adopt a child and are struggling to find a birth mother. Infertility has been on the rise for decades. And many people who are still single aspire to be parents. When you complain about parenting, how does that resonate with others?

It's fine to commiserate with another guy who's going through the same thing as you, but don't make it a habit with everyone.

Remember the good times and leave the bad times where they belong . . . in the past.

# CHAPTER 49

# Bad Boys, Bad Boys, Watcha Gonna Do?

For families, a pattern can emerge between spouses where one parent disciplines a child more than the other. It's especially true for the mother who stays at home, as she takes on the full responsibility of the child for the vast majority of the day. This includes the good and the bad, like special memories that represent the "firsts" (walking, talking, etc.) and the discipline required to correct bad behavior.

During the workweek or after an extended business trip, some guilt inevitably settles in when you finally return home. You don't want to dampen the spirit of the moment. This happens to many men, and you may find yourself explaining to your son why you are telling him to go in a time-out or gently nudging him to stop slamming a children's book on an ottoman after a dozen loud *thwacks*. You don't have to explain yourself to your child—you simply have to enforce rules.

If you pass the buck when it comes to discipline, this results in two outcomes: your wife will always represent the bad cop, and your son will simply start going to you when he feels the urge to behave badly. Besides, if mom's not looking, he knows he'll get in less trouble when he's misbehaving around you.

On weekends, or when explicit bad behavior is taking place when you come home, take over and be the disciplinarian. This maintains a united front, sets firm boundaries, and gives your wife a break. She'll appreciate the respite—God knows there will be days when your son has been a terror that she's had to manage alone for ten plus hours.

If this feels awkward or you feel any sentiment of guilt, imagine how this imbalance will exacerbate itself in three or four years. Your wife will end up being the only source of discipline in the house and you'll have less overall equality.

Most importantly, your son will respect you more if you enforce the rules.

# CHAPTER 50
# Solidarity Is a MUST

The minute your child realizes he can get what he wants from you when his mother denies him, it's game over. The manipulation game has begun, and kids are experts at this as soon as they put words and actions together.

If your wife disciplines your son by verbally raising her voice constantly, you should not step in the moment this occurs. If the roles are reversed, she should respect your authority. Children notice patterns, and they both respect and gravitate toward them; however, if there's a schism between you and your wife, they'll use that to their advantage.

Are you letting your son off the hook when he doesn't finish his meal, but your wife won't let him leave the table until he eats his dinner? The same level of discipline has to resonate from *both* parents. If your son acts up at the playground when it's time to leave and you give in to him so he can continue to play, how will your son act when your wife tries to enforce a certain time limit? You both need to espouse the same message.

The list can go on forever, but when it comes to the basics, more communication is always better. Speak in private or when your son is in bed for the night to ensure you're on the same page. Perhaps he's exhibiting a pattern of behavior that needs to be addressed and you and your wife disagree on how to manage it. Maybe you need to call a friend or relative for advice before deciding the best course of action.

Either way, a united front is paramount when you're striving to establish good behavior or habits. You'll accomplish a lot more together than you will as separate decision makers.

# CHAPTER 51

# The Teams You Love

You've been following them since you were six years old. You could name every player and recall the winning touchdown or home run that got them into the playoffs back when Bill Clinton was president. No one questions your love for Team X.

Your son is two years old now, just big enough to fit him in your favorite team's jersey. He's planted next to you on the couch, excited just to be with you, when your team is playing on TV. Your jerseys match, of course, because Team X is playing their biggest rivals in the division—they HAVE to win this game!

The opposing team gets away with a foul call. You jump to your feet and scream, "*What!?*" You hold back a litany of expletives by substituting words, but your blood is boiling. Then your team drops the ball and you're pacing the room, yelling at the television. Your wife said something, but you're too upset to even acknowledge her existence. Then your team's coach makes a bonehead decision and you're waving your arms in fury. *This is a travesty of the highest order!*

Your son is watching, listening, and perhaps mimicking behaviors he doesn't understand. From his perspective, his role model is yelling at a rectangular box that provides images of a team wearing jerseys that match the one he and you are wearing. He's processing this, and the net result will associate this experience with either passion or insanity.

There's a big difference between the two. Which one represents a healthier behavior to espouse and pass along to the next generation?

# CHAPTER 52
# The Family Meal

The best way to gain an understanding of what's going on in your child's life and how she is developing is over a shared meal. The easiest way to find out how your wife is doing or how she's holding up (either at work or as a full-time mom) is, again, best accomplished over a shared meal.

That meal should be dinner. A great time to recap what transpired with everyone is at the end of the day. Make this a priority as soon as your daughter starts to eat at normal times. It usually takes place around eight months of age, sometimes a bit earlier or later.

The family meal also helps your child develop communication skills. She can watch you share a conversation with your wife and learn the dynamics of interpersonal communication. This will set an important pattern in your child's development. You will be shocked by what comes out of your child's mouth when she's able to put words together and join in the regular conversations at the dining room table.

Children gravitate toward family get-togethers. It gives you a regular place to interact with your family and provide them an understanding of what's going on in your life. Your work—as either a stay-at-home dad or your job—matters just as much as your wife's.

The free entertainment provided by the family meal will also keep you grounded. The best antidote after a horrible meeting with your boss is watching your daughter eat a bowl of spaghetti for the first time.

## CHAPTER 53

# What Not to Include During the Family Meal

The family meal should not include two common elements that are part of our daily lives. On their own, they are useful, informative, and entertaining. But they are also a major distraction, so rule them out during family meals.

The first rule: *No technology at the table.* According to Dscout (a reputable digital research firm), the average American touches their smartphone 2,617 times a day.[1] Remove it from the meal. Putting down your fork every time someone messages you will interrupt the flow of communication, and the meal itself. It will also make your child want a phone when he or she is a toddler, and that's not the kind of message you want to send. Directing their interest to a three-by-four-inch screen will not provide the means to truly enjoy their childhood. There's too much for your child to explore and discover about the world at large.

The second rule: *Turn the TV off.* If it is on, at some point, all of you will turn to it. If the news is playing in the background, do you want everyone to snap their heads around when war footage bombards the screen? Do you want everyone's focus to shift to a gossip show espousing empty values about plastic surgery or how an overpaid celebrity is working through the challenges of bulimia? That's not the point of a family meal.

---

1   Dscout. "Putting a Finger on Our Phone Obsession." June 16, 2016. https://blog.dscout.com/mobile-touches.

Mealtime is about the three (or more) of you connecting, communicating, and understanding one another on a daily basis. More importantly, your child will see you and your wife getting along, working through issues, or speaking with one another.

That's a great message to send. Responding to another text won't make you a better parent.

# CHAPTER 54

# A Technology Rule for the Twenty-First Century

Technology permeates our lives at every juncture and is, without question, one of the most revolutionary developments in the past twenty years. The access we have to online content, educational tools, and digital social communities is limitless.

Technology is threaded throughout our work, social, and family life; however, the irony over the past twenty years is that our collective enthusiasm surrounding digital access has never been studied at length in regards to child development. Don't believe me? Search using the phrase "technology and the effects on children" and watch what pops up in the results. Not one single government-driven study exists addressing what may or may not be a concern. The children coming through adolescence today have been raised with unfettered access to digital outlets.

As adults, we have the means to impose self-discipline and control when it comes to interacting with digital media. Children do not. It's time for our society and today's generation of parents to ask themselves what limits to impose on our children when it comes to accessing technology.

If you need further proof, drive past any middle school and see how many children are staring at three-by-four-inch screens. Ask parents who have older children how frequently their kids access social media or involve themselves in texting, and you'll get an earful.

Here's one rule you can instantly apply when it comes to your immediate family: Use technology for educational purposes as an alternative to television once a day. For periods of boredom or when you or your wife need ten minutes to accomplish something, provide access to physical toys, creative outlets, or sports-related activities to children under the age of two. As they get older, you'll be able to provide them access to more advanced toys and the backyard. But for now, limit their time on a tablet.

As a fellow father once told me, the worst decision he made was to give tablets to his two children, both of whom were younger than five. It consumed all their attention and, when the battery needed recharging, the result prompted unending meltdowns.

He advised me to stick to "technology" that is better suited for toddlers: Play Doh.

## CHAPTER 55
# The Shared Ritual

I mentioned in earlier chapters that children gravitate toward schedules and patterns, and it's best to have positive ones for your daughter to enjoy. A shared ritual can serve a broader purpose: It will provide you with some level of redemption. If you are away during the day, you will have something to look forward to every day when you come home—focused, quality time with your daughter.

Set a daily ritual with her, one you and she will both enjoy. This could be something you enjoyed with your own father before he passed away, moved, or left your family. It could be a big hug the moment you walk in the door, or singing the same song to your daughter every night before you tuck her into bed. Maybe it's an Eskimo kiss or a back rub when you first see her in the morning. If you play guitar, perhaps it's a song you play and sing to her. It should come from you and be personal.

Pick something you can provide consistently. Years from now your daughter will grin every time she thinks about the ritual she shared with her dad. That's a terrific tradition to pass down from one generation to the next.

# CHAPTER 56

# Your Expectations . . . and Your Child's Life

**Y**our daughter may only be eighteen months old, but for some time, you've thought about what she will do and where she will go in life. This may have started before she was even born. Perhaps she will be an outstanding athlete or will graduate at the top of her class. You've thought about the path she will take, and you hope (on some level) she will follow in your footsteps. You've achieved something with your life; doesn't every parent want the same for his or her child?

You will see this materialize among other parents when your child enters preschool or starts to get involved with athletics. All parents have high aspirations, and they will express their pride when they see their children emulate something at which they excelled.

One can make the nature versus nurture argument. Some will say great athletes are the offspring of those who excelled at sports themselves. But what if a daughter isn't interested in the sport chosen for her by her parents? What if a great musician hands his son a guitar, but his child simply wants to have books read to him or use his imagination in other ways?

Rather than set firm foundations, why not provide a fluidity of experiences? Carve a shallow path before your child and see if her interests carve a deeper chasm, like a river through a forest. But let your daughter experiment, see what captures her interest, and nurture her passions in a less controlled manner.

Remove that mind-forged expectation you have for your daughter and see where life takes her. She'll find her passion, and if her talent and interest continue, she may find a way to turn that passion into a profession.

A wise person once told me, "Love the job you do, and you'll never work a day in your life." Provide your daughter the opportunity to figure out what she loves. That way, wherever life takes her, her job will be tethered to her true passion.

# CHAPTER 57

# The Overbearing Parent on the Sideline

They will be there, cheering on their child with reckless abandon while rushing up and down the sideline of whatever sport the children are playing. More often than not, it will be the father, whose ambitions in the sports world never materialized. Now, on this tiny field with three-foot-something little athletes scurrying about, this overbearing father will do everything he can to infuse his daughter with the spirit of competition.

. . . And make a complete ass out himself in the process.

Your daughter is far too young to experience this yet, but give some thought to how you and your wife approach your involvement in sports; it can include important life lessons and provide a treasure trove of memories for all those involved.

Your conduct on the sideline represents your desires and hopes for your child, but your daughter has to find her own desires and hopes. The father screaming at his daughter to run faster and try harder is simply setting the stage for his girl to resent him when she realizes it's all about him.

Be better than that.

# CHAPTER 58

# What It Means to Man Up—Your Time

**A** new way to think about free time is to represent it as a form of currency.

It's not very sexy, but if you equate time to currency (free time = more currency), you're a rich man before you have kids. The one common denominator that links all fathers to one another is the lack of free time when a child comes into their lives.

You were likely a rich man before your daughter was born. You had tons of free time to enjoy concerts, play sports, or pursue hobbies. Now you have to be more selective. The independence you enjoyed pursuing these interests will not completely end, but it's time to prioritize this part of your life.

If you're already in the first year of your baby's life, God knows you're aware of this fact. Take comfort in the fact that you'll get some more "currency" as time goes on because kids become more independent with the passing of years. Just consider your first year as a parent a sabbatical from the golf course or basketball court.

The point is, when you become a dad, don't shortchange your kid. The more time and energy you commit to being a dad will pay huge dividends down the road.

## CHAPTER 59
# Spontaneity—Just Do It!

If you wake up one morning with a grueling day of work ahead of you, experience a worse commute than usual, or have endured a ton of stress as of late, pause for a moment and consider a radically different approach.

Look at yourself in the bathroom mirror when you wake up, and before you shower, say the following phrase:

"Sometimes in life, you've got to say, 'What the f—?'"

If you don't recognize the phrase, it's from the movie *Risky Business*. It's a classic not to be missed. And if you find yourself laughing after you say the phrase, then open the bathroom door, tell your wife you're taking your son for a day trip . . . and go!

Pack a bag, make sure you have everything you'll need, pick a location, and hit the road. Take a day trip to the beach on the first warm, spring day, or go into the city to visit a park. See if there's a community event for kids in a nearby town and go with your son. Do a simple cursory search on the web for local events and find something . . . anything. Be 100 percent spontaneous and just enjoy the day. It's probably better if your child is older so he'll have more stamina, but more importantly, he will be overwhelmed with joy with the time he has to share with you.

Right before you take off, email your boss and inform him you have a stomach bug. The shorter the message, the better—otherwise, it will sound like you're BS-ing him or her.

And you are . . . to give yourself some quality time with your son. Just do it!

PART 4

Guest Interview #1

# CHAPTER 60

# Dana Glazer—Producer and Director of *The Evolution of Dad*

**D**ana H. Glazer is an award-winning filmmaker and father of three young kids living in northern New Jersey. An NYU Graduate Film program alumnus and Student Academy Award winner, he has written screenplays for Warner Brothers and the Syfy Channel. He teaches film at Fairleigh Dickinson University, produced short videos for *USA Today*, and writes for *The Huffington Post*.

His fatherhood documentary, *The Evolution of Dad*, was featured in *The New York Times*, on CNN, and on *The Today Show*. Mr. Glazer was also invited to the White House for a presentation of *The Evolution of Dad* at a fatherhood event. Mr. Glazer's latest documentary, *Parents of the Revolution*, is about activist parents in the Occupy Wall Street movement.

KENDALL: Tell me about your father.

DANA: I'm very fortunate to have a father who has been very involved in my life, and continues to be. When I was born, he was not permitted to be in the birthing room, which is interesting. I think that was indicative of the time. My father grew up with a father who said to my dad when he was ten, "Now you've got to be a man, and there's no more hugging and kissing."

When I was born, my father expected that I was going to hop out of the womb and play . . . basketball, hockey, and do all these things with him. In fact, he actually went and purchased a hockey stick and a football. That's what he was; that's what he was expecting in some sense.

The funny thing is that my father was never an athletic guy. He always wanted to be, but never really was. And so . . . when I was a teenager, there was some expectation. Why wasn't I practicing harder? We had a family psychiatrist who said, "Well, that's not how it went for you. Why does it have to be that way for him?"

My father had to figure a lot of these things out from not having a role model of a father. His dad worked at a car dealership and was gone most of the time. My father didn't have a strong father role model to work from. He had a hard time disciplining me when I was very young, and that's one of the reasons why we got this family psychiatrist to work with him—in terms of his understanding of how to be a disciplinarian.

My father actually had to learn that behavior . . . In terms of not just trying to just be my buddy, but to be a parental figure. It didn't come naturally to him. He did change course, which, for his generation, was pretty good. A lot of fathers didn't do this.

My father certainly wanted to be engaged. He was a lawyer and he worked full-time . . . [but] I never felt like my father wasn't around. He was very engaged with me. He instilled in me a passion for movies. He's not a filmmaker, but he instilled that love for movies in me.

I always felt that he was there for me, that he was there to take care of me in all sorts of different ways. I never felt like there was some lack, which puts me in the minority of people, because that's not usually the case. My parents have been happily married for over fifty years.

KENDALL: That's awesome.

DANA: I'm very lucky about all this . . . When I was about eighteen [years old], I set up a video camera to just record during Christmas morning, which is kind of funny, because we're Jewish. My mother comes from a background that's a mixed religious marriage. But watching this . . . it was just a camera that rolled for about an hour. Just seeing us interacting with each other unedited, and the amount of love amongst us, is really tangible. I was very fortunate to have grown up in a family that's very expressive in terms of love and affection.

It's been a lot of the way I handle my kids, given I had a strong role model with my father. I also had my grandfathers who spent time with me in different kinds of ways. Overall, a lot of love in my family and very fortunate, and now I'm passing it onto my kids.

KENDALL: That's great. So, let's change topics for a second. Why did you produce *The Evolution of Dad*?

DANA: I was inspired because I had a lot of confused feelings about being a father, because on the one hand, it was a life-changing, incredibly positive, meaningful experience; on the other hand, my career as a screenwriter was not going well. I was at home a lot, which was great. But [back] then, there wasn't that much social support for at-home dads, and I felt isolated. There was also a degree of, well, you're just not complete; you're emasculated. I think that still exists, this labeling that people do, or these associations that they have for dads who spend a lot of time at home.

There was a lot of confusion about that. A friend of mine said, "You should make a movie about that. Talk to different fathers and hear what their experiences were, and connect with different people."

It was a fun experience of trying to balance out being an involved father and making this film, which was very intensive . . .

Some time has passed and the film still gets orders from people and schools, and they're still using it in classes in over 250 different colleges and universities across the country.

KENDALL: Impressive.

DANA: It's not like the themes and the subject matter have changed so dramatically. It's a very slow-moving process. The issues of work/family balance, gender equity—none of these things have changed so dramatically since I made that film. In fact, with the political climate that we're in . . . there's a regression in play, so it remains topical.

KENDALL: You were, and you are, a stay-at-home father. So we understand, what were the family circumstances that led to that decision?

DANA: Let me just say first off, the "at-home-dad" name/moniker—I've always thought of myself as a "work-at-home" dad because I always thought the idea of an "at-home dad" is you're at home taking care of the kids (and doing nothing else) while your significant other goes out and works. It's not so cut-and-dry that way.

I actually teach college classes. I make films. I know that there are some people who'd be very happy just taking care of kids. Personally . . . purely doing that and nothing else would shrink my brain too much. I've always thought of myself as more of a "work-at-home" father, but I'm happy with being called a "stay-at-home" dad as well.

KENDALL: What were some of the most gratifying things when you were home with a two-year-old, and some of the challenges in your daily life?

DANA: I have a little bit of amnesia about that, given it's such a long-gone experience. I think that snuggling up with them certainly was a very exciting, wonderful thing. And when they had fuzzy heads when they were really little was special. When they would have these looks on their faces of discovering something new that they had never experienced before. I think that's the benefit of having kids . . . Everything becomes a little bit mundane, [but] for them, everything is magic. It's special. It's all magic. That magic rubs off.

KENDALL: That's very true.

DANA: To see things in some sense through their eyes is very gratifying . . . They're mirrors for us. I think I learned a lot about myself as a person from having young kids that I hadn't considered, because when you react to children, they're thermometers of truth. They react in kind. You have to really be thoughtful about how to work with them, too, because if you start screaming and yelling, it's all over, and that's damaging for them.

But, on the other hand, they're trying to test you because they need to know where the boundaries are. They want to be able to press against those boundaries. And for you to say, "Nope, that's where the boundary is," that's security for them. That makes them feel better.

My wife and I have had lots of conversations about how to discipline (what kind of things do you do, don't you do . . .) There are things that in the short term seem to work great, but in the long term are a bad idea.

I remember when [my son] was little, he would do something and I'd give him a little tap on the toosh. Then I realized I had to keep tapping a little bit harder for it to make a difference. I was like, "Why am I doing this?" Because I was, in essence, teaching him that hitting is okay, so I had to find another way. At a certain point (very early on), I said, "We're not doing that anymore; we don't hit." If there's . . . a mantra with the family, with the kids, it's: "We don't hit." It would be disingenuous for me to give him a smack and then say, "We don't hit."

[My wife and I] read books in terms of trying to understand how best to discipline the kids. There's a book called *Positive Parenting*, and it's an interesting read. For example, one of its questions was, "Do you prefer to have a child who is curious or a child who is obedient?"

It kind of goes back to the idea of the family as somewhat democratic, as opposed to the stern father who's not going to explain himself. We're firm, but whenever we do something and it's an overreaction, or we act badly as parents, we say to them, "I didn't handle that as well as I could have," and we discuss it. We try to encourage good behaviors, as opposed to being punitive.

You're not just teaching the kids to behave themselves; you're teaching them how to behave in the rest of the world, and you're trying to encourage them to think about what they're doing. It's a tricky thing.

Children need to have a degree of structure that's consistent, and that structure is time for you to [figure out] stuff. Otherwise, you lose your mind.

KENDALL: That sounds like a chapter in my book, *Rookie Father*. To seek out advice, be a sponge, take in opinions. You don't have to act on them. But whenever you can get an opinion as a new dad, take it and run with it, and just absorb it.

DANA: Sure.

KENDALL: How did your marriage ebb and flow in the first six months when you were a work-at-home dad? What about when you had three kids to manage?

DANA: The first is the starter kid. Then the second kid . . . that's when it becomes interesting. The third kid—now you're outnumbered. The first six months, I always think of as "baby boot camp," where you're not sleeping very much. You're basically acclimating to the kid and the kid is acclimating to you. You're basically trying to adjust your life, and if you've never had a kid before, that's a bit of a steep climb to try to get used to those [new] rhythms . . .

So in terms of the first six months, you're learning how to do all these things. That's not easy if you're a working dad. I think that dads are culturally programmed to be like, "I have to go work. And not only do I have to go work, I have to go work now, harder and longer, because we have to make more money now because of the child."

There are going to be all these costs. There's some truth to that. That becomes a point of contention for a lot of marriages, and often leads to divorce. That's a big problem.

Then you have the gatekeeping issue of the mom who says, "Oh, you don't know what you're doing." Oftentimes, if the father is not acclimated to the baby (to the cues the baby makes, the noises) and the mother is more acclimated, then she's like, "Oh, you don't know what you're doing." And then the dad says, "Well, then I'm just not going to do anything," which just leads to a lot of contention.

The trick with the first six months is . . . if it's at all possible, you take some time off [from work] when your baby is first born.

Where *The Evolution of Dad* is at this point, it hasn't really moved very much in the last fifteen years, in my opinion, in the sense that it used to be that fathers were not allowed in the birthing room. That was my father's generation. Now, to be in the birthing room is a badge of pride. I was there, we got the baby out, we did it. Then the dad goes back to work . . . At its best, most dads are out of work for two weeks, which, compared to the rest of the world, is pretty pathetic. There's no real support. The Family Medical Leave Act, which was created in 1993, does not support fathers. There's no incentive for fathers to feel better about themselves to stay at home, and so, it really is watered down. It's really dependent on company policies.

KENDALL: That's changing. In the ad tech space, companies like

Facebook and Google have had to roll out policies for dads just to compete with other companies to get the best talent they can.

DANA: Good. I'm glad to hear that.

KENDALL: Last question: Your expectations as a father before your wife was pregnant versus where you are today . . . what kind of father [did you think] you would be [and] what surprised you the most in terms of the reality of parenting?

DANA: If you don't have children, you have a lot more time for yourself. Once you have children, you have a lot less time. From the outside looking in, it's like, "Why would anybody want to inflict that upon themselves?"

But what you don't understand until you're going through that process is that the mundane experience of the day-in and day-out of being a parent, and being involved with your kids, has exponential meaning to it. As you get older, it gives value to your life that you didn't understand before.

. . . If I were to go away for more than a week . . . from my wife and kids, I think it'd be devastating for me because I would feel like a big appendage of my life was missing. But if you did that for two weeks, you'd be—

KENDALL: I'd be devastated.

DANA: Right. It's a very profound alteration if you're able to and willing to have the experience of being engaged with your kids, and with your wife, and really sink your teeth into that; it's very profound. If you go off to work and spend all your time at work, it's tragic. It's a tragic thing that people end up in their lives with this hole in their heart, and they only realize it later on . . . in some sense, they had cheated themselves out of the most meaningful thing they ever could have done.

# Safety and Structure

# CHAPTER 61

# Section Preview: Safety and Structure

**W**hether he's still in the womb, past the baby gate stage, or a toddler, you may not see the point of addressing safety and structure. For the time being, you and your spouse are already lifeguards 24/7. This section, however, is about setting a foundation for the years to come.

The goal represents a common denominator in and outside the house: **autonomy**.

This entire section lies squarely on the shoulders of the wisdom I procured from my mother-in-law when our son was just beginning to walk. Your instinct when a child is strong enough to lift and crawl under a baby gate is to protect them from anything that can hurt them. What happens when they are strong enough to lift that gate and crawl toward a fireplace or the kitchen?

A time comes in a child's development when you have to decide: hunker down and play defense, or educate your child for the benefit of everyone in the home.

If you choose the latter—educating—the first lessons will require at least two hundred verbal reminders to your child so he can understand the rules. It can be frustrating and mind numbing, but once he gets it, the rules stick . . . forever!

When we remodeled our home and the wall between the kitchen and the living room went down, it was not during my son's "wonder" years, but during his "wander" years. When I had a pot of boiling water on the stove, he sauntered in (knee-high) to see what I was doing. "Go back in the living room, please." When the stove was hot with a chicken broiling inside, there he was. When he reached for the bag of flour on the counter, I said, "What are you doing in here? I'm cooking. Out, now."

Then there was the fireplace, which we finished with glass-paneled partition doors. He could lift the baby fence surrounding it with one hand. He'd throw a ball at the glass panels and was strong enough to open the doors and access the knobs that controlled the automatic gas fire itself. "Stop throwing the balls in the house . . . Stop playing near the fireplace . . . Stop trying to smash the glass with that toy!"

The word "stop" came out of my mouth at least a thousand times in a three-month time frame. My stay-at-home wife repeated the word five thousand times! I think my wife started losing hair during the process. We were at our wit's end, but soon he could freely roam around the house because he learned what was unacceptable behavior. We educated him.

I speak from experience—educating children makes life easier.

# CHAPTER 62

# Autonomy Starts with the Ferber Method

**W**hether you're expecting or you're walking around with an infant in a stroller, stop by a popular playground over the next several weeks. Observe how parents and children interact with one another. At a certain age—somewhere around three—children often set out on their own within the confines of the area to play with other children.

If nothing less, it's entertaining to see what parents are doing at the playground. If they are not chatting to one another or participating with their kids, they are likely nose down in their smartphones. Sometimes too much, which is kind of pathetic. They spend so much time consumed with a three-by-four-inch screen, they miss the bigger picture in the distance—namely, their son or daughter's childhood. Don't be that guy when it is your turn.

More importantly, you'll also observe something else at the playground. Some kids will seem tethered to their moms or dads. They will appear glued to the father's hip or attached to their mother by an unseen umbilical cord.

The way to avoid this begins by espousing autonomy with your daughter, which should start early and can be achieved by practicing the Ferber method (which advises parents to let their children cry it out when they wake up at night). Time charts are available online. Although the process takes time, gradually the child learns to soothe himself to sleep.

When you have the opportunity to espouse strategies that encourage toddler autonomy, embrace it. If you don't, the flip side will be a child who always demands your attention and time to be entertained. This can be rough when neither parent gets a break over an entire weekend, let alone for the stay-at-home parent every single day of the workweek.

Encourage your child to "entertain" himself when he becomes a toddler, and try not to always rely on that crutch called the TV.

# CHAPTER 63

# Babyproof? Of Course!
# But Educate Too

It wasn't long after our son started walking that we had to address certain safety issues in our home that were driving us crazy. We babyproofed everything that came to mind (or was obvious), but certain factors remained a challenge. For example, our fireplace mantel (complete with glass doors) was concerning.

My mother-in-law shared the wisdom she procured over the course of raising three children: "Teach your kids not to play anywhere near the fireplace."

When our son was sixteen-months old and we had no way of stopping him from lifting and moving the baby fence surrounding our fireplace, we had no other choice but to try the teaching approach. Some days we had to tell him to move away from the mantle thirty to forty times, but he eventually got the message.

When we remodeled our kitchen, we opened it up to the living room. We were concerned our son would get too close to the hot stove, and a baby fence simply would not work. We received the same advice: "Teach your son hot stoves are very dangerous."

When he was two years old, we made sure he could feel the heat coming out of the oven from a safe distance. We said, "Ouch!" and pointed out how hot it could get. We repeated the phrase "Stay out of the kitchen" at least five hundred times. And he learned. Before he was two and a half, he stopped coming into the kitchen when someone was cooking. He was old enough to understand the consequences because we educated him on the dangers in the kitchen.

One time he grabbed an electrical cord tethered to a table lamp in our living room and yanked the plug out of the socket. We both made a big deal about it and showed him how fragile the glass base of the lamp was. "That could really hurt you if it broke! Ouch! Don't do that." After a dozen similar incidents, he knew not to yank on electrical cords.

This type of parenting, where you have to repeat yourself time after time, can be extremely frustrating . . . but it works.

Before the age of three, our son could safely roam around the combined kitchen and living rooms; he could play freely in other rooms with lamps and glass-door cabinets without a parent immediately present to make sure he was safe. He learned about consequences from the time he could walk.

If you take my mother-in-law's sage advice and educate your child in this manner, your life will be more manageable and worry free.

## CHAPTER 64
# The Helicopter Dad

As noted in the previous chapter, teaching your son about consequences can pay fantastic dividends. The same holds true outside of the home.

This book focuses on men who are expectant fathers or have a child below the age of two. So, yes, you should follow your child around the playground to make sure he doesn't try to climb a structure geared for five-year-olds. Absolutely nothing wrong with that.

There are parents, however, who are so concerned with safety that they become helicopter parents. They hover over their children and fuss about them so much that it becomes abundantly clear they have little to no confidence in their child's ability to make smart decisions.

By using the same process inside your home for the outside, you can avoid becoming a helicopter dad. When you're at the playground and your son is running full speed toward a wooden bench, stop him and point out the obvious. Show him how hard the bench is and how it would really hurt if he ran into it at full speed. If he's not holding on tightly enough when trying to climb from one object to another, show him where he would fall if he let go. Physically express with a facial or physical gesture the pain he would feel.

When he starts climbing a child-sized structure, show him how to climb it—one hand, one foot at a time—so he knows how to do it safely.

If he refuses or tries to ignore you, then playtime is over. Put him back in the stroller or car. Set the rules, use discipline, and stick to it. The next time he wants to go to the playground, reinforce the message that he has to listen to you or the trip to the playground is not happening.

You'll be shocked how quickly his listening skills improve because he knows if he doesn't listen, he'll miss out on a great time on the slides and swings.

# CHAPTER 65
# Check Small Things

In Colin Powell's book *My American Journey*, he included a list titled, "13 Life Rules for Any Future Leader." One of the rules was to "check small things."

He shared an example from his days when he served in the Eight-Second Airborne Division where his job was to double-check soldiers' latches to ensure they were properly tethered to a security line; when a soldier jumps from a plane, the latch triggers his parachute to open. One day Colin found his fellow soldier's latch was not secured to the security line. Had he jumped, he would have fallen to his death. Hence, check little things.

When you come home, check for little things as well. Is the button you forgot to pick up still in the corner of your bedroom? Is it a choking hazard? If your child is beginning to walk, is there a sharp table corner just his height?

Perhaps you rented a house for a family vacation with a spiraling staircase from one floor to the next. The banister posts on those staircases are widely spaced. Could your daughter slip through them if she climbed the stairs?

You don't have to be paranoid, but if you have any doubt or concern, say something. If it costs time or money to correct something before the risk translates into an accident, ask yourself what the time or money commitment would be if your girl were injured.

That should provide the resolve you need to do something.

# CHAPTER 66

# Bugs, Basements, and Pools . . . Oh My!

**M**ost of us cannot afford to live in brand new, spacious, modern homes. Some of us choose not to and prefer the character and quality of an older house.

Some parents (when home shopping) avoid properties with pools because of the imminent risk of their child's untimely death, or they may avoid older homes with unfinished basements because they aren't kid-friendly or kid ready.

Put your fears aside and take a mature approach if you're faced with any of these scenarios.

For those who live in older homes, or if you're considering a dwelling that has served several generations, I recommend two areas of focus: *cleanliness* and *insulation*.

More often than not, gaps exist somewhere in the structure of the home and provide free reign for insects and cold drafts to enter. Neither should be welcome when your newborn comes home from the hospital. Make an effort to plug holes, repair cracks in walls, and invest in new windows. You'll have less risk of disease from insects or rodents, and you'll save money by replacing outdated and uninsulated windows. Bring in an expert to check out the insulation of your home as well. That upgrade, over several years, can save you thousands of dollars.

When it comes to pools, a person could label them risky or dangerous, but they needn't be. If you and your wife are considering a home with a pool, put money aside to invest in a child proof pool fence and a tight-weave pool cover (for those in colder climates), and ensure the fence around your backyard is secure and up to code. When your son turns two, invest in swim lessons and stay with him in the pool when you use it. The lessons will pay off when he's four and swimming laps around you.

The rewards of a pool on a hot summer day are priceless. Pools are also a great way to entertain family and friends, which means the fun comes to you. You don't have to travel or drive before Junior is down for the night. This is exceedingly rewarding when you have a cooler filled with ice cold beers.

# CHAPTER 67

# Pets in the Home

**Y**ou may have married the biggest animal lover on the planet. Your two-year-old son may hug every dog within reach of his tiny arms. Perhaps you already have one pet and envision expanding your one-dog show into a full-on circus of pets to amuse and entertain your child.

Bear in mind one unwritten fact when it comes to extending your four-legged family: There's no guarantee how a new animal will respond to new surroundings and children. Everything may go well at the pet store and the animal may cuddle up to your son in a manner befitting of a heartwarming dog food commercial. But when you get home, this will be an entirely new environment for the animal.

Tap the brakes and wait until your son is three years old before you expand the family pack. It comes down to communication and your son's ability to understand both consequences and discipline. Both will be required to love a new pet. And before the age of three, your number one priority should remain centered on your child and not training your dog.

You have enough to manage when it comes to diapers, and pets come with rear ends that require constant servicing (i.e., poop bags).

## CHAPTER 68
# The Schedule

Something about children and structure really works. I'm not a psychologist, therapist, or a doctor, but I know setting up a schedule your child can rely on simply . . . works.

The opportunity appears when his sleep schedule starts to normalize. (When he moves off formula or breastfeeding and is able to sleep beyond four hours at a time.) When that moment occurs, it's time to get a schedule locked down and in place for the next several years.

The process is oriented around regular feedings, naps, and playtime. Although you don't have to schedule every moment of every day, certain elements should represent fixed time periods.

Breakfast, lunch, and dinner should all happen around the same forty five minute time frame for each meal. This will give your daughter an understanding about when to eat, rather than snacking or eating whenever she wants. When she gets older, she'll learn the reciprocal scenario. If she doesn't eat during the time allowed, she is going to get hungry and frustrated. This will motivate her to eat. It also saves a parent the frustration of stopping whatever he/she is doing to accommodate Junior's hunger pains.

The same goes for naps. They should start and stop around certain times, depending on your daughter's needs. Naps represent the unspoken parental treasure: free time! Encourage your daughter to keep napping.

If your daughter starts waking up at the crack of dawn, go to her room and ask if everything is all right. Even if it's 6:00 a.m., tell her it's the middle of the night and to go back to sleep. Sometimes this works if she's groggy, and you can enjoy another hour of sleep as well.

An established schedule will also help you find time slots when you can accomplish something, such as an hour-long trip to buy groceries. A schedule helps everyone in the family.

PART 6

## Your Work Life

# CHAPTER 69

# Section Preview: Your Work Life

If you put your job before your family, you will miss your child reaching a number of milestones. If you don't earn enough money, you'll miss the opportunity to upgrade to the life you hope to achieve, but it may require business travel and more time spent at the office (and away from your family).

That's the rub . . . and in cases where both parents have to work to afford a lifestyle of their choosing, it's further magnified. For many of us who do not have a connection with our own fathers, there may not be a blueprint to follow on how to manage this challenge, which is more difficult today than it was in the past. The income from a single breadwinner used to be able to afford a comfortable house, cars, and family vacations. Today, with health-insurance premiums, college loans, and the expenses of having a child, two incomes are often not enough.

So we work harder and longer—checking emails late into the evening, getting to work earlier, making sure the boss has what he/she needs. Those who earn fantastic money (and are not in the medical, financial, or legal fields) work in fast-paced industries that require more from workers than ever before. I'm willing to bet the hours we put into our commutes and jobs is greater than what laborers in the past endured before unions existed in the 1800s.

Let's be honest: Our take-home pay is all we have to work with. What one chooses to do with that money says a lot about a person. Furthermore, when one generation starts to emphasize other parts of their life outside of work (namely the millennial), rather than labeling them "lazy," we should jump on their bandwagon. Maybe we can find a happy equilibrium—a goal the baby boomers never achieved.

*The number one job a parent has is being home and present for their children.*

Another element distinguishes successful parents: They know how to manage their take home pay. They save for their children's education, their home, and their retirement, and only thereafter do they consider material upgrades. Regular trips to Starbucks and buying German-made cars should not precede the need to be thrifty, save, and invest in the long term.

Manage your work life to provide for your family in the long term, and manage your money in the short term to afford everything you deserve later in life.

# CHAPTER 70

# Organizing Your Work Hours

**W**hen you watch your favorite athletes play, take note of their focus when the game is in play. Their eyes are on the court at all times. With the exception of baseball, even players on the bench are attuned to what's happening on the field of play.

When the game clock is ticking, there is little to no downtime. Now that you're a father, ask yourself if you bring that same focus to your work. Are you stepping out for a coffee with coworkers? Yapping about the game last night for twenty minutes? Are there things you can do to be more productive? Doing so will afford you more time with your son at night. Feel zero shame in leaving work at 5:15 on the dot every day to see your child if you've spent every hour leading up to that time focused on your job.

Here are seven tips for anyone with a nine to five job:

1. **Set Realistic Meeting Times.** If you control the calendar for a meeting, why schedule thirty minutes if you can flesh everything out in twenty? Push your subordinates or anyone involved in the meeting to get to critical issues quickly.

2. **Purpose/Process/Payoff.** If you're a manager, start every meeting by stating the goal of the group's conversation (purpose), what it will take to accomplish the goal (process), and the decision that needs to be made (payoff).

3. **Limit Short Breaks and Lunches.** If the cohorts sitting

next to you speak ad nauseam about his/her kid, bar outings, or whatever, excuse yourself physically or wear headphones to drill down into your responsibilities.

4. **Synchronize Travel Plans.** If you have to travel to different regions in the country for business, condense those trips whenever you can. It will provide more evenings with your son.

5. **Hit the Eject Button.** If your presence in a meeting or a conference is not mandatory and you're not getting real value from being there . . . leave. If someone voices his or her concern, inform them of a bigger priority you're tasked with and then take care of it so you can get home to your son.

6. **Weekly Reports.** Why write four sentences when it can be summed up in two? It may sound like common sense, but if you're inputting multiple points, it takes less time to read and edit. Your boss may appreciate that too.

7. **Next Week's Task Sheet.** On Friday afternoons, bullet point what needs to be tackled the following week. When you return to work after the weekend, you can start tackling each item one at a time. Prioritize them from top to bottom.

Managing your work life properly will result in providing your child with a present you may not have received from your dad on a daily, or even weekly, basis. That "gift," per se, is your presence. Doing this will ensure your daughter's memories feature you as an active participant because you were *present* when those memories were cemented during her childhood.

# CHAPTER 71

# The Clock and Your Ambitions

**Y**our employer, wife, friends, and coworkers never question your ambition. A wide swath of people like you have great expectations for themselves. That's nothing to be ashamed of.

Your ambition may not even be wholly centered on your career. Maybe you're a competitive runner and you want to participate in an Ironman Triathlon in the next few years. Maybe you've got a fantastic concept for a business you were ironing out before your child came into the picture. These side endeavors or ambitions are the fuel that drives you.

But a career, parenting demands, keeping up on the social front with family and friends, and special projects and goals can empty your fuel tank pretty quickly. Your free time gets squeezed from a multitude of commitments.

It comes down to the clock.

Even if you are lucky enough to get eight hours of sleep, once you subtract work, being a dad, and commuting, you don't have much time left. So here are two suggestions on how to manage your time:

1. Set a time to leave work every day that gets you home in time to see your kid. Leave the later hours to subordinates and junior personnel, or get back to that work project *after* you spend dinner with your family. Plan to share thirty minutes (at minimum) with your kid every night, even if that sacrifices your time in front of the TV. This brief window of family time is critical. That bond

with your son or daughter is magnified with each and every moment you spend with them.

2. For those other ambitions—whether it's the Ironman Triathlon, tennis, writing, etc.—adjust the time when you go to bed and when you set the alarm clock: one hour earlier on both ends. The first hour of the day translates into quiet time for you. Mother and baby are sleeping, coworkers are not emailing one another, and clients are still comatose. Use that time for yourself. If you need to work out at the gym in the morning, add another half an hour and go to bed at 9:00 instead of 9:30, then wake up at 6:00 instead of 6:30. There's nothing dishonorable about going to bed early when you're a dad.

This process will likely cut into your time in front of the TV, the tablet, and maybe the smartphone. Good!

Collectively, as a country, we're addicted to screens. It's not a bad habit, but think about how you can spend that time to your own advantage.

I wrote a novel in two months by getting up at 5:15 every morning. I could then hit the shower by 7:00 to get ready for work. It took another year to button it up, but consistency got me through it. Your mind will adapt to the change of pace and hours. You will be shocked by what you can physically and cognitively accomplish once you commit to a schedule.

Or you can sit around at night and watch reruns with your wife.

Set that alarm clock, dude . . . tonight.

# CHAPTER 72

# The Boss of Your Family

If you've got a high-intensity job, guess who ultimately holds the biggest influence when it comes to you being able to spend time with your family?

Yup, it's that person in the slightly bigger office to whom you report. And he or she may have high expectations that could affect your role in your family. Your boss may be a parent as well, but if push comes to shove, she will prioritize her family before yours.

Thankfully, that is changing because of the millennial generation and we, as a country, should be grateful for it.

You can approach this touchy subject with your boss in a few ways. For example, if your boss designates you to start taking more cross-country business trips, this will impact your role as a dad. You have to start setting boundaries, but you can't position it as a "won't"; instead, label it as a "can't." If both you and your wife work, you honestly may not be able to deliver on all of your boss's wants and needs.

Another way is to let your boss earn her paycheck. Your boss is a boss for a reason. She likely has many others reporting to her, and it is her responsibility to figure out a strategy on a broader level and work with those under her according to their availability/schedules. Don't be accommodating to the point where you sacrifice seeing your son before he's unconscious for the night or only during the weekend. You should see him every night, or four nights at a minimum, during the workweek.

More importantly, he needs to see you.

# CHAPTER 73

# Your Boss and Your Limits

**A**t 6:15 p.m., she hands you a folder and asks you to take a look before her 10:00 a.m. meeting tomorrow. A forty-five minute commute home awaits you, and (if you're lucky) you might get fifteen minutes with your son before his bedtime . . . IF you leave right now.

Your boss notes that it's a senior-level meeting. "Sorry for the short notice, but . . ."

The unspoken truth persists. In her mind, the company comes first, despite the fact she knows you became a dad less than six months ago.

You always try to get out the door at 5:30 in order to be home in time to see your son before he nods off to sleep for the night. You're feeling squeezed between your family priorities and work responsibilities. This is inevitable for millions of new parents. For Gen X and millennial parents who change jobs more frequently than past generations, the issue is exacerbated. With each new job comes a new boss and a new challenge to prove oneself professionally.

It boils down to the culture of the company: Is it family-friendly or not? We don't consider this before having children. But once you're a parent, things change on the work front, and it's worth considering a three step process.

First, you need to man up and have a one-on-one with your boss. Your life has changed, and that means your family comes first. If tackling an assignment or project requires more time, mention you will come in earlier when the situation requires it. If you've got other time-sensitive responsibilities, ask her what the priority is for the company. Flip the script: Make her decide what your number one focus needs to be. But be sure to explain that you have to leave work in time to see your son before the day ends.

Second, if others report to you, train them to assume broader responsibilities. They don't have to do your job per se, but there's no reason not to delegate certain tasks to them. Run the idea by your boss and fib about your main objective: increasing productivity.

Third, get your resume buttoned up and start networking outside the company. Make it a priority to attend industry functions, seek other people out, and engage them in talking about their business. Dive deep into LinkedIn.com, if you're not already there. Start connecting and follow up to see if potential employers can share a cup of coffee before work. It's worth taking the time to do so because the net result may provide you more time with your family.

And make sure you ask one important question during the interview process: "Is your company a family-friendly environment?"

Then listen—closely.

# CHAPTER 74

# Mothers' Rights are Paternity Rights, and Paternity Rights are Fathers' Rights

If both you and your wife work, chances are the company she works for will provide a paid maternity leave as part of her package. That's the law, which was authorized by Congress in 1993 under The Family and Medical Leave Act.

The total number of states that provide fathers the right to paid family leave, or paternity leave? Five: California, New Jersey, New York, New Hampshire, and Washington D.C.[1] That is inexcusable.

The issue of fathers' right to paid paternity leave is starting to change in certain industries. The ad tech world is taking a lead position, due in part to the competition to attract and hire qualified professionals.

The laws of the land will not change immediately, but there is momentum. The long-term solution is electing officials who support paid leave for new dads. It's a no-brainer; there's no reason why fathers shouldn't have the same rights as mothers.

If you are not provided paternity leave, here are two suggestions to secure as much time as possible when your child enters the world:

---

1   "What are the Laws Around Paternity Leave and Family Leave in the U.S.?" Fatherly.com. June 4, 2020. https://www.fatherly.com/love-money/paternity-leave-laws-state-us.

1. Request two additional weeks of vacation shortly after your wife's first trimester when you share the news of her pregnancy. Couple that with whatever time off is regularly available to you, and then include whatever paternity time off your company offers. This should total three to four weeks compared to the alternative, which is likely two weeks off, at most.

2. Present the request, both in person and in writing, so that you have an opportunity to note your recent achievements. This represents the starting point of the conversation, which may result in a negotiation. If you start by spotlighting your successes, you will put your request in the most positive light.

You have nothing to lose except time with your newborn, and you should take note of how your company manages the situation. If they take the position that they cannot afford to offer this benefit to everyone at the company, keep the conversation centered on your wife and child's needs. Reinforce that your request relates to owed vacation time and you are not asking for the company to change its overall policy. Your fallback position should be an assurance you won't take paid time off for a set period of time upon your return from work, which may help to sway any lingering concerns.

Don't be afraid to ask for something that will help you be a better parent—ever.

PART 7

# Guest Interview #2

# CHAPTER 75

# Alan Katz—Former Publisher and Media Titan

Over the course of my career, I've had the pleasure of working with a number of fantastic executives. During my tenure at Condé Nast Publications—one of the top media companies in the world—I worked with Alan Katz, the former vice president and publisher of *Vanity Fair* and *Cargo* magazines. Besides his work ethic, charisma, and intelligence, he is also a terrific father to three children and remains happily married to his wife, who also works in the publishing industry.

He started out in the publishing world at *New York Magazine*. Over the next fifteen years, he worked his way up the corporate ladder to the role of publisher. Despite travel demands, long hours, and intense competition, he was a committed family man. One of the keys to his success was his ability to manage his work life, family life, and all his hobbies while holding senior positions at high-profile media companies.

Alan's perspective represents someone who was able to balance fantastic success during his career and family life. Here is his story.

KENDALL: Tell me about your dad.

ALAN: My dad was a great guy. He was super funny, smart, and loved music, travel, and food. He did not come from much and his parents were immigrants from Russia. They didn't speak very much English at all. His father escaped persecution and fought in the Russo Japanese War.

KENDALL: That was in 1904.

ALAN: He was born in the late 1800s. They immigrated to Brooklyn, which is where my father grew up. He had five sisters. He was the center of that family, being the only boy. Very funny, very charming, and received a high school education. He also served in the Navy in World War Two and was very proud of that. He served willingly and fought in the South Pacific.

I have his diary from then. A kid who had never been out of Brooklyn saw so many amazing things. His handwriting started getting shaky midway through the diary. Reading it, you can see a wide-eyed kid turn into a very concerned adult. He witnessed battles, saw death, destruction, and even saw a kamikaze hit his ship. Very interesting stuff. He was [raised in a Jewish home that practiced the Orthodox traditions] and prayed every day.

[He was] always a music lover. He had an encyclopedic knowledge of music, especially jazz. He ended up getting into the record business [as] a record salesman, and then did that for the next twenty-five to thirty years. He began collecting 78s (records) and then LPs (vinyl). I had his 6,000 LP collection, but sold them about ten years ago.

He worked five days a week for the record company, but on Saturday, he had his own business. He would go into the neighborhoods of Brooklyn, primarily black neighborhoods where they couldn't get credit to buy from the majors.

He'd load up his trunk with the records of the day, not his own label, but any of them he knew—like James Brown, Marvin Gaye, the hits they wanted—he'd sell them piece by piece to these little record shops.

KENDALL: Wow.

ALAN: I used to go with him on those Saturdays to the Brooklyn shops. I was able to see this other world. It made me feel great about my how dad didn't see color and was there to help them, but also, of course, to help himself have a business. It was a wonderful symbiotic relationship. I would often play with the sons of the shop owners.

KENDALL: You have siblings; tell me about your relationship with them.

ALAN: I have a brother and a sister. My brother's six years older and my sister's four years older.

KENDALL: You're the youngest.

ALAN: Yes. My mom died when I was eight, so I had a single dad for a number of years until he remarried. Because I was the youngest, I spent a lot of time with him . . . at work, shopping, movies, breakfast, and luncheonettes.

Back then, in the '60s, my siblings could be more independent, so he had to look out for me. My dad put me under his wing more than not, and I was happy to do so and be with him. We'd go to movies together. Sometimes he'd cut out in the afternoon and we'd go see a double feature in the village. We'd go to various shops. I loved going to the record stores and thumbing through 45s (singles), posters, and albums. I have so many great memories.

KENDALL: When you lost your mom, who in your life, outside

of your dad, stepped up? Were there relatives? Was it the synagogue?

ALAN: Excellent question, and the answer is almost zero. No one stepped in and no one stepped up, save my mother's father, [who was] also an immigrant.

KENDALL: Really?

ALAN: My father was a very private guy. He was big, he was boisterous, funny, gregarious. But he didn't like people in his business. The one person who [helped] was my grandfather, my mother's father. He lost his wife [too] . . . and made it his mission to visit us as often as possible, bringing kosher chickens, challah, and cakes. But we were in Long Island and he was in Brooklyn and didn't drive—ever.

KENDALL: He was from Russia.

ALAN: He was. My mother's father was the classic networker. He helped people come over [to America] . . . He was a beachhead and here to help them, get them jobs, get them a little money to start, and send them out into other areas. He was very well liked, very well loved. A very serious man. He assimilated more than my father's parents. He somehow got into banking, and while he never was a major banker, he worked at the bank and had a lot of relationships through that.

But my grandfather, right away, stepped up monetarily to help us. He sent me off to summer camp. My mom died in April. By June I was off to camp at eight years old, not knowing where I was going, not knowing a single person. But he knew the guy who owned the camp. My grandfather was probably seventy years old then, yet was still working.

He worked until he was ninety-one years old, then he had a stroke and died at ninety six.

My sister stepped up. She filled that motherly spot for me and always has. She absolutely stepped up.

KENDALL: How did your father parent? Was he disciplined? Strict? How did he manage the three of you?

ALAN: He was fun, but very strict. He was an interesting guy. Liberal thinker, Democrat, gregarious, fun, funny, and he knew the music scene. Yet at home, very strict. Very old school, Depression old school. My mom also was very strict.

"I'm not your friend, I'm your father." That would be a very important line in my youth.

KENDALL: I like it.

ALAN: I liked it a lot, because we knew where the line was. We would have fun. We'd fool around. We'd wrestle. But if you touched his ear or his nose too much, if I was saying something too flip, he'd say, "Hey, I'm not your friend, I'm your father."

KENDALL: Given your dynamic, were there times when you and your siblings had to look out for one another? Were you a latchkey kid growing up?

ALAN: Yes, one hundred percent. We never had a babysitter. My mother was sick for many years before she died. There was a nurse that came in and she would cook sometimes. I was probably five when my mother got sick, and eight when she died. When left alone, we might have cereal or frozen TV dinners. Chicken Delight was big in my home. "Don't cook tonight, call Chicken Delight!"

We were latchkey kids, one hundred percent.

KENDALL: Tell me what you loved about your father.

ALAN: He was funny as hell. Somewhere between Buddy Hackett and Don Rickles. He looked a little like Buddy Hackett. In his later years, [he] got very overweight and was a little bit round. People didn't think of it as a bad thing back then; you just thought he was a jolly guy. To me, sweet. To me, very strict.

At the dinner table in the later years, I was developing my sense of humor, being the wise guy a little bit. And if it wasn't funny enough, he would put his fingers together to form a zero.

KENDALL: Probably made you a little sharper so you could come up with something faster.

ALAN: Probably. He was very fast and very animated, and had some good shtick. And a lot of phrases. I picked up a million phrases from him.

KENDALL: Did you feel any anxiety when you found out you were going to be a dad?

ALAN: Of course. *Who am I to be some kid's parent? What do I know? Am I going to be good at it? Am I going to be strict when I need to be strict? Am I going to be lenient when I need to be lenient?* I didn't think my dad was perfect, but I appreciated him. So, yes, I had lots of anxiety.

KENDALL: What do you rely on from your youth and your family experiences to raise your children?

ALAN: My dad and my mom. I can't leave her out because of those eight years she was around. She was artistic. She was philanthropic in a sense that while we didn't have money to give, she worked rummage sales and . . . at the temple, things like that. She very much looked out for others.

I have an art streak in me, and she fostered that. But she was also incredibly strict. She was also a great dresser, and so was my dad. She always had cool outfits. Everything was an outfit . . . And she was smart. She was the smartest one in the whole family. They always said that. She had a cultured ness to her.

My father had this thing about making promises. He would never make me a promise he couldn't fulfill. If I said, "Dad, are we going to go get an ice cream cone later today?"

He would say, "Yes."

I'd say, "You promise?"

"No."

"Why not?"

"Because I'm not sure if we're going to be able to do that today."

I learned not to make a promise I couldn't keep. I try to do that with my kids and friends, and in business.

KENDALL: What values did your dad possess that you cherish, that you tried to pass along to your own kids?

ALAN: He had a great sense of fun and sense of wonder. I got that from him.

To be open-minded, to love music, to love the arts, to love TV and film, to care for your brother and sister. My brother and sister—having lost both parents—had other issues through their lives . . . We've stayed together throughout.

We're very different people, all three of us, but we're still together. We used to do every birthday together and every Jewish holiday. We instinctively knew that we had to stick together or else there's nothing. It's very easy for people to have nothing. They split up, especially after divorces or deaths.

Kids don't stay together with their siblings. We're very different people. I wouldn't say we're always the best friends, but we're always together. I think that's from our dad.

KENDALL: After your first daughter was born, did that change your perspective on parenting? Did you know you were having a girl?

ALAN: Yes, we knew her gender. One of the biggest fears I had of being a parent was [the thought] 'Is my child going to be healthy?'

I became a very doting father. I took her around with me everywhere. You can talk to clients who, to this day, remember me showing up on a Saturday morning at a store opening and there she was with me, strapped to my chest. We took her everywhere.

We didn't stop our lives initially. It's a recommendation I give to younger people today. Everyone's always afraid your life's going to stop when you have a kid. You hunker down, you never go out. We chose to do it differently. We'd have dinner with our friends and bring her in the car seat. We went on holidays, we took her with us. We went on business trips, we took her with us. We always incorporated her.

She made our lives better and more interesting in seeing everything through her eyes. She was ridiculously cute, and we had fun.

KENDALL: How did you both manage three kids?

ALAN: Transparency. At the time, I was a publisher of *New York Magazine*. Cheryl was at *Self* magazine.

KENDALL: High-octane jobs.

ALAN: Yes, but well-oiled machines . . . We had a lot of connections. Unfortunately, Cheryl's mom passed away shortly before Olivia was born. We got a baby nurse who was with us for the first couple weeks. Then we got a nanny who came in. Cheryl went right back to work, so we both learned what we needed to know on how to hold her head while you're bathing her, feeding her, and everything. We did have outside help. We were fortunate . . . we figured it out.

KENDALL: If you're speaking to someone who's about to become a father, or a man caring for an infant, what are the three most important pieces of advice you'd give them?

ALAN: First one is, as a father, no one tells you that the first three months the baby doesn't look at you, doesn't know you, doesn't care about you. It takes about three months for them to get over the fact that the mother's [not] the only thing in the universe and to really look at you. When that hits, at three months, it's the coolest thing in the world.

[Second,] have kids sooner rather than later. You don't want, necessarily, to be an old dad. I'd say have a kid when you want to, which is earlier.

Kids make your life better by and large. [They] fulfill something that you didn't even know you needed. As someone shared with me, you've done all the running around, you've traveled, you've gone to all the clubs, the bars, but it's important to have something in life that's not about you, that puts a lot of perspective on the world and your life. It's a really good perspective to have when you're younger, I think.

[Third,] kids don't really need a lot. Kids don't need every toy. They don't even need their own room. They just need a little corner with something—[like] the box the toy came in—to play with. That makes them happier, which is another thing my father taught me. I learned, as a father, you don't need as much as you think you need economically . . . Give them the time. Be there. Be present. They'll change you more than you think you're going to change them . . . We learned quickly to be less fussy as parents.

But look, my father wasn't perfect. Luckily, I learned from his mistakes. He wasn't always there for us. He wasn't always present. He didn't make it to all the school functions and the baseball games. After he remarried, [he and his wife] didn't foster a feeling of togetherness . . . She was more anti-social. So I vowed to be more open to and for my kids. To make sure they went out for all sports, all school plays, whatever they were passionate about. And most importantly, to make the time for them, to be there, to participate.

Never say, "I can't do that because it doesn't fit my schedule."

KENDALL: What would you have done differently as a parent if you had to do it all over again? Mistakes you made and the lessons you learned along the way?

ALAN: I would've started younger.

KENDALL: Really?

ALAN: Paramount. I would've started younger. I was the opposite of what I just said. I was still building my career. I was at *New York Magazine*. I wasn't a publisher yet. I was concerned fatherhood would curtail the fun I was going to do, that we didn't have enough money. So I would start younger, because as you get older, you need more money to do certain things. It's easier, earlier on.

When [our daughter] dropped her pacifier, we'd wash it off, sterilize it, or throw it away and get a new one. Then we'd go to visit our friends who were around kids a lot; their daughter was the same age as ours. Things drop on the floor [and] the mom puts it in her mouth, gives it back to her. She's crawling all over the yard. We're like, "Oh, we totally have this wrong."

They're resilient, kids. They can handle dirt. Kids can handle whatever it might be. Leave them alone. Let them be kids. Stop being that fretting parent.

KENDALL: You achieved a lot of success in your career. Where did your source of motivation come from, and where did you acquire your work ethic?

ALAN: I probably acquired my work ethic from my mother and father. Specifically, my father, who worked six days a week—five days for the man, and one day for him. He found time to work hard, to have fun, and do cool things.

I wanted more. I wanted to earn the respect that I felt I deserved. I wanted to make more money. I wanted to have more access to things. I guess my work ethic came from that point, came from what I saw around me, and what I didn't have compared to what I wanted. And then, I went after it.

I wanted to be a leader, not a follower, so I worked toward that. I read things in business books, magazine articles, newspaper articles, and I got a lot from movies. I just went after them on my own. When they were successful, I repeated them.

My work ethic also came from that line my father said, "If you love what you do, you'll never work a day in your life." I was always seeking to love what I did so that I didn't feel I was working.

People would often ask, "How many hours do you work a week?"

I was like, "I don't know." It was all the same to me. Many days were nine to eleven at night. My work ethic came from just making my work my life.

KENDALL: Two more questions. What's the secret to a great marriage?

ALAN: I think friendship. I think it starts with finding common ground and always working towards it. It took me too long to learn it's better to be together than to always be right. You have to like hanging out together. My wife and I have always loved hanging out together. We often like the same things or picked up things from each other. Common ground, respect, friendship. All of those build on each other. And, obviously, physical attraction, which—well, you know why.

KENDALL: What's important to keep in mind if you want to be a great father and husband?

ALAN: It's really important to be present. Really important to put your heart into it. In the later years with my kids, I became their soccer coach for all three . . . at different times. I never played soccer in my life. I never watched soccer in my life. I didn't care about soccer. But I knew that that's what they were doing on Sunday mornings, and I wanted to be there.

I went to the first couple of games and realized I want to be a part of this. I coached soccer for over ten years and still, to this day, know very little about soccer. But I have to say, I was a really good coach. I love running into kids in the neighborhood I used to coach.

I loved it, and I love the fact that we'll always have that time together. And to be honest, it helped me be a better manager in business.

. . . I think one of the hardest bits is giving the kids enough room to be themselves, but still being strict enough to keep them on the straight and narrow. More conservative than liberal. I may be incredibly liberal in my political thinking, but incredibly conservative as a parent. Everything from holding the fork the right way, holding the pencil the right way . . . you sit up straight at the table, bring the food to your mouth, [not] your mouth to the food. You have to put your feet down, you don't sit with your legs up. Kids are way too casual these days. We didn't do that as kids.

That was something from my father. He would also say, "When you're out of the house, I want people to think that you grew up well. You didn't grow up in a barn."

He always made sure that we did the right thing, ate the right way, stood the right way, spoke the right way, looked people in the eyes, shook their hand. I guess that's a proper upbringing. Act at home as you would or should in the world and it's second nature. You won't have to think about it.

All of those things—etiquette—I got that from my parents, [especially my mom], and I've made a very big deal about it. Even sometimes being at odds with my wife or telling my kids' friends how to act in my home.

We also, as parents, started with no toys in the living room. In our small apartment, we didn't want stuff all over the house. You have a big enough room, you have enough toys. You have enough bins to keep them in, [so] keep your toys in your room. The house is not one open toy field.

But I think "I'm not your friend, I'm your father" is something that I've really lived by, as well as wanting to be a part of their lives. They say . . . that kids don't turn to drugs as much if you have dinner with them as often as you can, if you're a part of their lives.

We always want to know who their friends are. It's unacceptable if we don't know who their friends are. As they've gotten older, it's been harder. But we try to do things together and say, "Hey, bring your friends." Have [their friends] in the house and look them [in the] eye. Let them know who you are so you can hunt them down if they mess up! Ha!

Try to stay involved in their lives. My daughter is at college. We text almost every single day. Not in an annoying way. If she's busy, I get nothing, or she'll call [or] Face Time me.

"Hey, Dad, what's up?"

"Nothing. What are you doing?"

"Oh, okay. I'm almost in the dining hall. Bye."

We didn't say anything. But we did, didn't we? You know what I'm saying?

I think staying involved in their lives is enormous. Being a part of their lives is enormous. That's all that matters, and they know you care. Even if you're annoying, they know you care.

# PART 8

## Your Finances

# CHAPTER 76

# Section Preview: Your Finances

I watched my mother pace back and forth in the dining room. She appeared overwhelmed and confused. She saw me and sat down to compose herself, and then she broke down in tears.

"I don't understand, and I'm sorry you have to see me like this. But I don't know what to do," said my mother.

I was twelve years old, watching my mother melt down in front of me. I went to hug her and told her everything would be okay, despite not having any idea what she was talking about. I vividly recall this moment since my mom was a very strong woman and rarely displayed any emotional weakness. She finally settled down and looked me in the eye.

"I don't know what we're going to do, but I'm not sure if we're going to be able to keep the house." Then she cried again.

My jaw dropped upon hearing this. When one's childhood home—its very existence—becomes an issue, it's a memory that's hard to forget. What came next brought on an avalanche of concern.

"I have not received your father's child support check and we don't have the money to pay the mortgage."

Sadly, I knew exactly what she was talking about.

On a recent trip to Florida to see my father, he mentioned

that his new family—his second wife and infant daughter—represented a new circumstance that would change things on my end. He told me (rationalized) that his new home, mortgage, and financial circumstances meant my mother would have to carry on financially without his help. I received this news before puberty.

All I wanted to do was spend time with him and get to know my new half-sister. I loved her, and the trip for me meant an even deeper connection with my father's side of the family. Being an only child, having a sibling two thousand miles away was better than having no siblings at all.

Before my father shared the news about how he was going to stop financially supporting us, I observed him scooping up pocket change from the dashboard of his van. He mentioned he had opened a savings account to pay for his daughter's college education. Then he left me in the van while he went to deposit the pocket change in the bank. I can't recall if I asked him if he was saving anything for my college education. Perhaps I was too afraid to ask.

So my mother wept and worried. And I, her twelve-year-old son, shared the news about my father's decision and how she was completely on her own to deal with the mortgage and other costs associated with raising me. At that exact moment, I inherited paranoia about money and the fear of not having any.

The upside to all this was that when I entered the workforce, I was motivated to make and save money, and also very interested in avoiding the situation my mother faced. I wanted to make sure my future family was financially secure.

My mother netted out in life with a solid retirement plan—the result of thriftiness, a state pension, health insurance, and a small inheritance from her mother. She espoused an independent streak from an early age and throughout her golden years.

She taught herself how to manage a home and make repairs without the cost of hiring handymen or contractors. My mom bought books on how to repair electrical and plumbing problems. She painted every square inch of her home, multiple times, wherever she lived. She questioned every single expense, cut corners, and had the good fortune of relatives who helped her financially until she found a state job with benefits. She got through it all and passed along her wisdom to a child who only asked twice during her lifetime for financial assistance.

(For the record, the first time I asked was when I had just joined the workforce, but my mother told me to get a second job. The next time I asked, she agreed to help, but then I backpedaled—the thought of taking a loan from a relative didn't sit well with me.)

When money becomes a source of tension within a family, it can result in short- or even long-term consequences. Between now and eternity, spouses will bicker and struggle when it comes to the subject, so because this book is centered on preserving and strengthening one's family, it's worth sharing advice that can remedy the struggles couples face when they bring a child into the world.

This section is about how you and your wife can set a foundation to **excel** financially. You have a secret weapon: each other. Two parents, with a child in tow, are stronger together when they have a long-term financial plan and are both on the same page when it comes to savings and retirement. The quicker you embrace a plan and put it into action, the quicker you can reach your shared goals. Committing to the savings goals I recommend in this section will help you avoid challenging circumstances, such as a lost job, pay cut, and special educational or therapy needs for your child.

Together you can weather the storm that inevitably shakes the foundation of every marriage. I hope you'll lean in and embrace what I share in the chapters ahead.

# CHAPTER 77

# Financing Your Priorities

**M**ost people do not talk about money. It's not a topic that comes up too often in conversation, and for good reason. There's a fine line between bragging about what one has bought, or reciprocally, asking someone how he/she could afford the item in question. Frankly, it's rather obnoxious to do so unless you're speaking to a relative or close friend.

Placing this subject in the context of this book, most new fathers have not procured (in terms of knowledge) an understanding of how to set long-term financial goals. There's no shame in that; you've got a lot on your plate with a daughter on the way or a two-year-old sleeping in his crib.

For most of us who were raised without a father in the home, you may not have had a role model who set long-term financial priorities. At a minimum, your mom or grandma might have given you some words of wisdom about the value of saving, or perhaps you had a single mother who ran a tight ship when it came to expenses. The latter is more likely; moms have traditionally controlled the purse strings when it comes to household expenses. Today, single moms also have a better understanding of investing compared to past generations, given the online resources available and the increase in college-educated women.

The following represents a strategy of how to approach money that will help you finance your long-term goals. I call this new way to look at money the "Bucket Strategy." (This has no connection to the bucket list, a reference about doing everything you want to do in life before you die. That's another list you can prepare during your golden years.) This strategy will afford you the chance to do whatever you want when you retire.

Here's where the bucket reference comes in: Money is like water, and if you're like 99.9 percent of us, you want to keep as much of what you earn as possible. You need buckets, or long-term financial goals, to separate and hold that water to keep it from spilling and washing away into a sea of credit card debt or car loan expenses. These buckets hold the money you've earned and are allocated to critical goals.

Furthermore, some buckets are more important to save for than others. As one bucket fills to the top, the water spills over and another bucket catches it before it's lost. One priority is achieved, and then the next bucket (priority) is filled.

I'll speak about each bucket in a moment. First and foremost, to make any of this happen, you need a job. Ideally, this will represent not just a place to work, but a *career* that provides an opportunity to grow and take on greater responsibility. A career often goes hand in hand with a higher salary, which comes in very handy in terms of saving for your future. If you're in a dead-end job, think about related industries with better growth prospects. The financial demands placed on you down the road are only going to grow, so don't be afraid to investigate new opportunities.

With that in mind, here's a breakdown of how to prioritize your savings through the Bucket Strategy, starting with most important and ending with the least:

1. Your home
2. Living expenses
3. Retirement

4.  An education for your child
5.  Vacations
6.  The upgrades

Bucket number one is your home. If you live in a shoebox, prepare for every square inch to be taken up with toys, memorabilia, and crap that accumulates quicker than you would ever expect. A child's needs fill a vacuum, which (in this case) is the space between the walls of your home.

A one-bedroom rental or a cramped single-family home is not going to cut it very soon. You will need more space quicker than you think. So the first and biggest bucket is the need to find a bigger pad for your family.

This represents the biggest expense, month in and month out, that you'll have to manage.

When you find a spacious dwelling to call your own, it brings bucket number two into the equation: living expenses. Moving to the suburbs? Great. Now you have to buy new tools and equipment to manage the property. Things often break when you own a home, so you will need an emergency fund to fix major repairs, like a broken water heater. It's important to keep $18,000 to $28,000 (in present 2021 dollars) parked in a savings account for unexpected costs. That represents an important part of your living expense bucket, and it will cushion the blow if you have a major and unexpected repair project that requires a plumber, roofer, etc. This bucket also affords wardrobes, utility bills, groceries, clothing, and other monthly expenses.

Car financing/leasing falls into the living expenses bucket. Before you pick up a Porsche Cayenne as a second car, wait until you work through the next four buckets.

The next priority, before anything else, is your retirement fund. Yes, it can be daunting—where should you invest? How do you get a handle on all the available options? Should you hire someone to manage your money? This is also challenging because you are saving for an event that is likely twenty-five to thirty-five years away. Chapter 79 provides some basic investment advice, but here's one rule to live by: If you have access to a 401k, you can invest a maximum of $19,500 (as of 2021) yearly, and you need to max that out every year. Not including taxes or service fees, your retirement 401k will grow exponentially with a basic investment plan. Assuming a modest growth rate of 4 percent, your retirement fund will equal $575,445 before your daughter leaves college (twenty-one years of annual contributions, plus compounded growth, not including taxes).

The added benefit is that the money you save in a 401k is tax-free. No better option exists out there for the average worker. This enables you to shelter a chunk of your income from federal taxes. Those without access to 401k savings plans provided by their employer might qualify for an IRA account, which also represents a tax-free investment opportunity.

At this point, you may be asking yourself where all this money to afford the new home and retirement is going to come from. Back to the first point I made about your career: The Bucket Strategy at this point gets a lot easier if you make more money. If you earn a raise or find a better paying job, it will help to fill each bucket as you move down the line.

The next bucket represents saving for your child's education. According to Savingforcollege.com, as of 2021, the cost of college for your newborn by the time she enrolls will be $266,561 dollars (in an out of state/public college).

You are likely saying, "WHAT!?!" Welcome to parenthood . . . and don't freak out. If you start early and achieve a 4 percent savings rate in the market, you need to save $500 dollars a month after your child is born. Believe it or not, doing so will enable you to save nearly $172,000 by the time your child starts college. The sooner you start, the easier it is to fill that bucket month in and month out.

You may ask why saving for retirement is a higher priority than saving for your daughter's college education. The answer is simple: Your number one priority is setting you and your wife up to retire at a reasonable age, in good health, and with enough money to cushion the blows that come with aging. Your daughter has the potential to secure scholarships, grants to pay down loans, and take on some debt if necessary. You're raising a child to become a productive member of society and be mature enough to manage whatever financial headaches come with adulthood. Your headache later in life should not be trying to figure out how to pay down a mountain of college debt when you've earned your retirement.

Next up is vacations. This doesn't have to include exotic safaris or stints in Waikiki. It can represent family weekend trips, jaunts to amusement parks, or a long weekend in the Caribbean. Getting away from your house, your job, and the daily grind doesn't just benefit you; it benefits your entire family. You likely have terrific memories of taking trips with your family.

When it comes to young parents, millennials represent the most well-traveled generation ever to roam the earth—so keep roaming! Prioritize this and save money to afford the opportunity to take vacations. If you save $50 dollars a month, by the time your child is four, you'll have $2,400. That can afford a week's vacation in Florida, assuming you're not staying at a four-star hotel or renting a luxury SUV.

The final bucket represents the "upgrades." This relates to the phrase, "Keeping up with the Joneses." For example, your neighbor, Bob, has a brand-new SUV with Wi-Fi, but you drive a ten-year-old minivan. You mow the lawn yourself while Bob pays a gardening service to take care of all his landscaping needs. A younger coworker looks like he walked out of a GQ photoshoot and your modest wardrobe is in dire need of an upgrade.

You know in your heart you deserve what those other guys have. Besides, you have a few thousand dollars left from the bonus you received last year.

Put conspicuous consumption aside, stop chasing a marketer's dream, and get your feet on the ground.

If you go down that road, your buckets run drier, your travel fund shrinks, and then your kid's college savings get dinged. If you add two new luxury cars into the equation, it inevitably drains your retirement bucket in the long run. If you want to sign up for big problems, pay for all those upgrades you want now and you'll have no money left over to buy a home or find a bigger place to live. That sixty-inch LED TV you want will still be there in six months, so don't fret—it's all about the buckets. Achieve each goal, from first to last, and then decide what you'd like to splurge on for yourself and your family. Then you can enjoy whatever you buy.

Most importantly, talk about these goals with your wife. Set priorities, stick together, and share the same goals across the Bucket Strategy. It enables you to completely account for her needs and will result in less fighting about the number one thing couples fight about: money.

Give time to let compounding and growth work in your favor. In twenty years, you'll find yourself affording your daughter's college, reminiscing about wonderful family trips, looking forward to retirement, and sharing all of this with that fantastic woman you call your wife.

Because you did it together.

# CHAPTER 78

# The Fundamentals of the "Bucket Strategy"

If you got through the last chapter and think you have it all figured out, then you're ahead of the game. More likely than not though, you're wondering, "How can I put the Bucket Strategy to work for me?"

If you're starting at ground zero, here's the next step:

When you boil it all down, you need at least four separate banking/investing accounts to get going. Pinpoint the figures you'll need by breaking down your paycheck into living expenses, mortgage/rent, retirement, your child's college fund, travel, and the "upgrades."

You and your wife should have one checking and one savings account. Checking is for living expenses only, and right before the end of the month, it should be close to zero. That reflects smart budgeting and managing your money wisely. Savings should represent your mortgage/rental costs. That account should also be close to zero after you pay this bill, which is likely the largest bill you pay each month. Divide your paycheck accordingly through direct deposits and shift money between accounts to pay the mortgage or rent.

Speaking of checks, go 100 percent with electronic payments. Stop banking like your grandpa. It's easier, saves time, and helps a family better manage balances and payments. Furthermore, consider using savings apps, like Mint, which can help a family budget their finances.

The savings for your retirement should go straight from your paycheck to either your 401k or allocated as a portion to a self-service brokerage account (E-Trade or Schwab, for example). Allocate retirement savings every time you get paid, either through direct deposits or by transferring money from your checking account.

You can also set up a 529 account, which is a program to help save for college. Research this option: Most states allow you to deduct money allocated toward a 529 account. The money you put into a 529 is after taxes, but you can withdraw money to pay college expenses tax-free. Translated, whatever money you invest in a 529 can grow without Uncle Sam dinging you on the backend. Start building both those nest eggs for your retirement (first priority) and then for your child's college education (second priority).

The last allocation should represent a second savings account. This is for travel and your "upgrades." Tie both savings goals together to simplify the process, and note what the money is for.

Most companies allow employees to deposit into multiple accounts. With this plan, you'll need to create four allocations or rules for direct deposits. If you do this every pay period, you're on your way to a solid financial foundation. If multiple deposits are not an option, sit down once a month and transfer money directly yourself.

You can always course-correct a few months down the road if you're a few bucks short in one account or another. If your response is, "I'll get around to it," trust me, the money you were supposed to save will evaporate quicker than a pool of water in the Sahara desert.

And you'll be left with an empty bucket somewhere.

# CHAPTER 79

# The Investment Battle Plan

**Y**ou have decided to stoke the fires in your 401k (or your IRA) and it's time to focus on your nest egg. Wise choice. But if you don't know where to begin, allow me to share my advice on how to approach it.

A key reason to do this right now is you may have one parent or divorced parents with separate long-term needs. Married couples have a built-in cushion. They have each other. Your parents may have faced bigger challenges come retirement time if they never remarried. Medical bills and long-term care may have wiped out whatever financial savings they had, despite Medicare coverage. It's safe to assume you may receive nothing in terms of an inheritance, so you and your spouse need to prepare accordingly.

Figuring out how to invest one's retirement savings can be a daunting task. If you have dabbled with some mutual fund investments or taken advice from a friend, that's fine. But now that you're a father, you need to set a foundation for long-term investing.

I promise no guarantee of impressive returns on your investments; however, if you stashed your money in a savings account that earns less than 2 percent, you're simply making it harder for yourself in the long term. You need structure and a process to diversify your portfolio as it grows to insulate yourself against the highs and lows of the stock market. You can speak to a thousand financial advisors, and if there's one core piece of advice you'll receive time and time again, it's the need to *diversify one's investments.*

I will explain how to do so, and the easiest way is through a football analogy.

You need a strategy to play offense with part of your money to grow your overall net worth. You'll also need part of your portfolio to play defense so a sudden market drop doesn't set you back too far. Regarding the types of investments you make, buying one stock and pouring money into it is the equivalent of investing all your money into a free-agent quarterback (which is very expensive). One player does not make a team, nor does one investment represent a financial strategy.

If you are starting from scratch, the best investments to begin with are low-fee mutual funds or ETFs (exchange-traded fund). These provide immediate diversification, as they focus on buying a multitude of company stocks. Most 401k plans offer a selection of investments, but if you are starting an IRA, you'll need to research and select these yourself.

You'll need several investments to start with, so here's how the football analogy works when it comes to building a successful strategy.

At the core of every football team, on both sides of the ball, are your linemen. If your defensive or offensive linemen are weak, it puts pressure on other parts of the team (i.e., the wide receivers, cornerbacks, your quarterback, etc.).

**Your "linemen" investments.** These should represent your core holdings: well established companies, otherwise known as blue-chip stock investments. You should also include dividend-oriented investments into this mix. These products (mutual funds and ETFs) invest in companies that have a history of high-dividend yields. The rule of thumb is to build around this category first.

**Your "offense" investments.** These represent investments that will outpace traditional options compared to dividend or large corporate options. For the record, these pose greater financial risks, but you're not going to get anywhere without including high-growth opportunities in your portfolio. These represent foreign or emerging economy-based mutual funds, like high-growth sectors that specialize in areas like biotech or nanotechnology. You could also include real estate investments (REITs) or mutual funds that specialize in vertical industries.

**Your "defense" investments.** These are exactly what they sound like: safe and secure investments that provide a balance to your "offensive" investments. Your number one safe asset is cash. Unless the entire world economy blows up, cash in America today is the simplest and safest way to save. When you add bond investments into the mix—and perhaps gold or other precious metals—you layer in additional diversification and security. Cash, bonds, and precious metals represent core defensive assets. Bonds, in particular, often fluctuate in the opposite direction of stocks. This represents one of the best ways to insulate your overall portfolio.

In terms of specific investments to buy and how to choose amongst thousands of investment options, do some homework to find highly recommended ETFs or mutual funds from well-respected sources. You can also compare and contrast investments when you open a Schwab or E-Trade account. Take your time and commit to the process.

If you are just starting out, begin with a simple savings account and wait until you have $10,000 saved. Thereafter, open up a money market investment account at one of the two companies noted above, or find another well-respected online financial institution that enables you to manage your money.

In addition, one should consider allocating the percent of money one has to make in each type of investment, so let's move back to the football analogy. Linemen represent broader (and lower risk) stock and bond holdings, offense represents growth, and defense represents bonds, gold, etc.:

| Conservative | | Aggressive | |
|---|---|---|---|
| Investment Type | Percent Allocation | Investment Type | Percent Allocation |
| Lineman | 50% | Lineman | 45% |
| Offense | 25% | Offense | 40% |
| Defense | 25% | Defense | 15% |

If you're close to forty years old, increase the percentage of defense-oriented investments to insulate what you have already saved.

*When your retirement fund equates to $250,000 dollars, seek an expert.* Hire a financial advisor and they will take you to the next level. Most advisors make money on the value of the entire portfolio, and to be blunt, most won't give you the time or oversight necessary to make a significant difference until you have a sizable portfolio to work with. They can help manage your money and diversify according to your age and retirement goals.

The key is to **invest consistently**, so consider automatic deductions from your paycheck to your Schwab/E-Trade account. Use the same strategy when you hire a professional.

Lastly, if you need further perspective on just how impactful this approach can be, consider what the result will be if you save $500 a month over twenty years. Let's assume a 5 percent growth rate (which is a conservative figure). When you take compounding into effect, here's the net result of what you'll have saved:

Annual savings: $6,000

Growth rate: 5 percnet

Twenty years: $225,031

Do you want to be a millionaire? It's not impossible! It just takes commitment.

# CHAPTER 80
# The Hot Stock!

It may have come up during a friendly conversation at work. Perhaps a friend with a cousin in the finance business suggested buying into a company that is about to go on a run.

You're confident this will happen. Your retirement fund needs a boost, you just cashed your annual bonus check, and everything you read points to quick gains and a fast buck.

Don't count on this to happen . . . *ever*. Many souls who were not on the inside wonder in retrospect what happened when that choice stock they heard about drops 30 percent in value. Unless you are working for a large and well-established financial firm, you will always be on the outside in terms of knowing where the market is headed.

In a broad financial portfolio, there is a place for prospective stocks. Think about holding these stocks for longer lengths of time to match your financial goals. If you buy, you'll never know the right time to sell, and your day job and parenting demands will inhibit you from making the right decisions at the right time.

As noted in the previous chapter, if you're a single investor on your own, look for broader-investment products like ETFs and mutual funds to stake a claim. If you have a financial advisor, let him/her earn his/her paycheck, which will allow you to focus on what enabled you to earn that bonus—focusing on your day job and being a great dad.

# CHAPTER 81

# The Least Exciting, but (Maybe) Most Important, Thing to Do

**Y**ou are likely old enough to have had a reoccurring expense appear on your credit card or in the mail. The bigger ones sit there like a wart and cannot be removed until the terms or contract come to an end. They also soak up the extra money you hoped to have at the end of the month when you wanted to splurge on something else.

Many of life's expenses represent reoccurring costs, but if you want to achieve long-term financial goals, you must take a long-term look at your family's cash flow. If you and your wife do not figure out a game plan after you bring your newborn son home, at some point, concerns about checking account balances, complete with a screaming baby, a run to the store for diapers, and a bad day at work are going to result in a fight about money.

Once a year, you should work on a budget game plan. Lay out your earnings and compare them against living expenses to see where you stand. This will result in fewer arguments about money.

Budgeting is straightforward. Gather all your bills and note down each expense and the corresponding cost in a separate Excel column. Account for miscellaneous expenses, like Starbucks coffee, apps you buy, etc. Include your rent or mortgage. When you have them all arranged, sort from highest to lowest, then add them up and compare the total to your total net income after taxes. This will provide a picture of your cash flow.

After you sort them by highest to lowest cost, work on the list from the top down, and then from right to left. Prioritize the bigger expenses (top/down), and see if you can find ways to reduce each expense (right/left). Double-check reoccurring expenses; is there anything you can live without? Now that you're parents, is it worth the convenience of spending $200+ per month on a cable bill? Can you reduce the cost of your cell phone plans? How much did you spend dining out? And don't forget to include automotive insurance costs. That may prompt the question: Do you really need to own two cars?

The result of all your effort may be an extra vacation. Money can't buy happiness, but it can afford better options.

# CHAPTER 82

# It's Not About How Much Money You Make, It's About How Much You Save

**I**f that's not clear enough, allow me to share an example I encountered during my career.

She was one of the more successful and hard-working salespeople I came across when I was employed as a media planner in the advertising industry. I was less than a year into the job and, as was often the case at the time, sales representatives would invite media buyers like myself out to lunch. We went with my boss to a fine lunch in New York City, where we all worked at the time.

I had no doubt this woman had her act together. She was smart, attractive, charismatic, and in her early thirties. During our conversation, she mentioned she had recently been promoted and given a raise. She talked about an upgrade she made in her living arrangements, which was renting a new, one-bedroom Manhattan apartment. She likely had a good reason to do so, as studio apartments in Manhattan are tiny, and her career trajectory was on the upswing.

She mentioned, however, her increase in income simply paid for that upgrade. It left her no room to save money, and she didn't know where she would net out in the end.

I thought a long time about that lunch, which was likely at a four-star restaurant. Her company provided her with an expense account that paid for the meal. When one is making $18,000 a year in Manhattan, as I was at the time, this lunch equaled a gift from heaven. A $2.00 slice of pizza was all I could afford.

At the end of my first year in advertising, I managed to save a paltry $800. I invested the money in stocks and, out of pure luck and timing, my investments grew to $2,000 dollars in less than nine months.

So where did things net out for me in that particular year, compared to the sales rep who was ten years older and likely earned six times my annual salary? Did I save more by living modestly with three other roommates and investing my savings? I'm willing to bet I had more money in the bank than she did by year's end.

Ask yourself what you will do when your next promotion or salary increase occurs. Will you splurge and spend on something you don't need?

Here's something you may encounter at your job: The new employee who was just hired out of college makes $40,000 a year and reports to you. Perhaps he is super thrifty, uses coupon apps, and lives with his parents. He manages to save $6,000 dollars in his first year . . . that's greater than what you saved, yet your salary is twice his. Maybe this "rookie" employee is better prepared for the future than you, despite being fifteen years younger.

That's kind of pathetic, don't you think?

# CHAPTER 83

# Cash Speaks Louder than Words

**T**rue in some cases, but not all, the expression goes, "Money is the root of all evil." Money is the number one cause of angst in relationships. Expenses, bills, and the exponential costs of raising a child can cause monthly, if not weekly, friction between husband and wife.

The easy answer (almost too easy) is to reign in expenses altogether. You can find obvious expenses simply by reviewing credit card bills. But here's a concept to consider: Pay for everything over the course of one month in *cash* and see if you stay within the budget you've imagined.

Going 100 percent cash provides a real perspective on the money you spend. It's easy to swipe your credit card and forget about daily costs until the statement is due. Using cash exclusively puts a real price on everyday costs when you physically hand over dollar bills to pay for everything.

Over the course of one month, agree with your spouse to exclusively use cash and discuss what you paid for from week to week. You may find that weekly trips to Starbucks, times two, turns into a monthly expense north of $100. Diapers, formula, and baby clothing represents an area you can't cut back on (unless you look for sales or use coupon apps). You may find the checking account after five, ten, or two-dozen withdrawals has nothing left for the last week of the month.

The process will reveal blind spots in both of your spending habits. Drill down on how you can work together to save money.

It's better than stressing out and fighting about credit card bills. This process may improve your family's management of money, which, in turn, may lead to fewer fights about the subject.

# CHAPTER 84

# That Ever-Elusive American Dream

Talk to someone from the baby boomer generation and you're likely speaking to someone who fulfilled the "American Dream."

They bought a house for $15,000 in 1978, and today it is worth $400,000. They traded in their Pinto in the late '70s, and today they have two foreign luxury cars in their garage. Their Social Security check—which they may be a few years away from collecting—is based on an under-funded system that is banking (per se) on the future income generated by Generation X and millennials.

Plus, that baby boomer bought a second home in Vermont, and he or she plans to pass the property down to his or her kids. How nice.

They had the world handed to them, provided by the "Greatest Generation" (the term Tom Brokaw used to define the previous generation, and is the title of his book). They consist of our collective great grandparents who endured the Great Depression as children and then went on to win World War Two.

The baby boomers had the world at their doorstep, and they benefited tremendously. We appreciate what they accomplished and their quality of life every time we sit down to a Thanksgiving meal in their spacious and comfortable home. They were either our parents or grandparents.

We do not have it so lucky and we never will. Today's parents who want to make the same material upgrades and give their kids a great life likely have to reset their expectations. We are learning the hard way, unfortunately. Too many of us in Generation X were crushed during the Great Recession when we upgraded to that dream home in the 2000s before the economy tanked. The millennial generation accumulated too much college debt, and a slower overall economy left an entire generation with high-loan payments. The dreams of millions were put on hold, and we've been recovering ever since.

I'd like to propose a safe bet anyone can achieve if they save and set long-term goals. Consider it a revision of the American Dream: The goal for the next generation of parents is to take the lifestyle you grew up with and raise it one notch higher. Just one single notch.

For example, if you lived in a row house, set a goal of going one step higher. Strive to afford a home with a backyard for Junior. If you were raised in a two-bedroom townhouse, buy a modest Cape Cod. If you grew up in a tiny split-level home, upgrade to a Colonial (one that provides a little more room to spread your wings).

That goes for everything. Maybe your parents drove a station wagon; buy a mid-size SUV with satellite radio. If your family took one modest vacation a year, take two or go on one annual trip abroad to give your son or daughter a taste of Europe or Asia.

The "American Dream" sits on a pedestal, seemingly out of reach for too many Americans. Your job as a dad is to move your family one notch higher, and maybe your grandkids will enjoy a lifestyle that is truly heads and tails above yours.

How does that play out in the long run? Junior gains a great set of values, a solid college education, and a pair of fiscally-responsible grandparents. Take a generational approach and you'll raise the game for generations to come.

# CHAPTER 85

# The Family Sacrifice

The obstacle to own your own home looms larger for parents today compared to any previous generation. Insurance, college loans, healthcare, and automotive costs have increased unchecked for two decades while incomes have remained flat. But that shouldn't stop you. Whining gets you nowhere, and every parent similar in age faces the same challenge. Those who persevere and overcome this challenge will be better positioned than most in the long run.

If you and your wife want to own a home—a fantastic goal—there's one single way to make it happen quickly (within one to two years), even if you do not have the financial means to make the down payment. It's a sacrifice you will have to make, and it's not pain free.

If you or your spouse's parents live close to where you or your spouse work, move in with them, if they are open to the idea. Pay them a modest rental fee, set your goals, and bank every dime you can for one to two years. If your family represents a two-income household and you both commit to limited spending, you can likely save enough money to make a down payment. If you represent a one-income family, it may take longer, but sacrifice what you can (premium wardrobes, the second car, the vacation, etc.) to achieve this noble goal.

This may represent a burden to either of your parents, but perhaps not. Your offer to pay a modest rent is fair-minded (because you're not a freeloader). If only one bedroom is available, it will be cramped, but more than likely the older parents may be thrilled to have a baby in the home once again.

This process will also require deft handling and diplomacy. Everyone needs to set their boundaries, especially older parents who are more set in their ways. Respect yours or your spouse's parents' needs—they are helping you save money to buy a home, which is no small thing.

The price you bear today, mentally and physically, will pay dividends when your realtor hands you a set of keys to your *own* home.

# CHAPTER 86
# The Financial Lifeline

**W**hen you buy a home, your next immediate step is to provide yourself with the means to access capital quickly should an emergency arise.

This suggestion may not make sense now, but given the investment you just made, which may represent you and your wife's entire nest egg, you're likely strapped for cash. A home is often the biggest investment a person ever makes, but in an emergency, where will the money come from? Asking your parents to borrow twenty grand when they are close to retirement and intent on traveling the world puts a damper on things.

A home equity line provides you the means to access cash on your terms.

This process essentially turns your house into a giant ATM; however, what if your wife is in a car accident, a tree branch takes down the roof of your garage, or your son requires unexpected surgery and insurance won't cover all the expenses? The home equity line of credit represents a source of money.

You're also in a fantastic position to set this up for your family. You've been vetted, approved for a loan, and now own a valuable piece of property, which is leverage you can put to use.

The best news? It costs little to nothing to open a line of credit. It can remain untouched for years, and accessing it is as simple as shifting money from one account to another (if you use the same bank for direct deposits and paying bills). If and when you do carry a balance, you may be able to write off part of the interest come tax season.

If you set this up within several months of buying a home, it will provide peace of mind. If you delay and your credit rating takes a dip, your ability to open a line of credit will be affected, and you may have to pay a higher interest rate.

Make yourself one promise on the back end: *The line of credit is only to be used in the event of an emergency.* That will keep you grounded.

# CHAPTER 87

# The Most Critical Two-Pronged Financial Strategy

**A**mericans have a problem with how they manage their money. We go from one season to the next, and one year to the next, without aiming for core long-term financial goals. If there's one goal that's critical, the topic I discuss in this chapter is it, and it represents a two-pronged approach: paying off your home.

In an earlier chapter, I discussed the first long-term savings priority, which is retirement. The next is saving for your child's college education as soon as he/she is born. You'll see a payoff when you successfully manage both saving goals in tandem with one another.

When you buy a home, you'll likely consider a thirty-year mortgage. This provides enough time for you to manage the costs from month to month (and the bank earns a tidy profit on the loan they made to you). Your time horizon for paying off that loan should not be thirty years; it should be twenty-five, at most. Here's why:

The overall interest you will pay for your mortgage is reduced significantly if you can pay off the mortgage in advance. You'll receive no penalties for paying down your principal every year, which, in turn, will reduce the overall interest you pay to the bank. Excluding home maintenance and repairs and insurance, the property taxes you will pay will represent your only additional financial cost.

Multiply your monthly mortgage payment (sans property taxes) times sixty. This figure represents what you'll save between the twenty-fifth and thirtieth year. It is likely a considerable sum. Usually all one has to do is to make one additional mortgage payment per year to make this happen. It may not be easy, but you will be in a terrific position at a critical point in life.

Here's the second half of the equation. Owning your home outright in twenty-five years will coincide within a few years of your child finishing college. Creating a 529 savings investment and saving every year will help to pay for your child's college education. If you have a second child and save for his or her college education, you're probably working with a twenty-five-year time frame.

Consider that moment twenty-five years from now, as opposed to thirty. Your children's education is paid for, your mortgage is paid off, and your children are likely entering the workforce. You now have more money to save and enjoy, and the home (which you will own outright) has hopefully appreciated. If you profit from selling your home, the derived income may represent a tax-free gain, which will add another layer of comfort in your retirement years.

If that sounds like a good plan, make it happen.

# CHAPTER 88
# One Last Hurrah

**Y**our wife is expecting.

A great change is about to unfold, and you and your wife are making plans, preparations, and readying for the new addition to the family. Excitement abounds! However, by the middle of your wife's second trimester, you will both go through a nesting stage that consumes most of your time. It will come like an avalanche when your wife is in the third trimester.

When your wife starts rubbing her tummy like a gypsy's lantern, that's it.

Looking forward to that Sunday NFL game at the stadium? I hate to break the news, but babies trump tailgating.

If you're somewhere between that first week and third month, you've got one last chance to get away. I keep bringing up the subject of travel because it's one of life's greatest pleasures.

Lay down a plan for one last great trip, the one that's been nagging at you for years. You can rule out African safaris or serious long-haul flights—they and pregnant women don't go well together. Vietnam is getting tabled, my friend. Perhaps it's a destination like Hawaii, the Caribbean, the Sienna region in Italy, or something as simple as a trip to visit relatives in Arizona. If the latter rings a bell, break away for a few days to see Sedona, or take a jaunt to the south rim of the Grand Canyon.

The first day your child sets eyes on you is the last day your eyes will have the chance to see a new corner of the world (for the next four to five years, at least).

So make your last pre-baby hurrah together count.

# CHAPTER 89

# Banking on Scholarships

If you or your spouse was a prominent athlete in high school or college, athletic scholarships may have crossed your mind when you started thinking about your child's college education.

Everyone knows the odds on getting a scholarship are not great, but the anxiety of saving a gargantuan sum of money can cause people to look for easy solutions.

The problem at hand relates to the human condition: We are frail and delicate physical creatures compared to many animals in the wild. Concussions, broken bones, torn ligaments—the list is endless.

Our unique, natural advantage is our mental ability, and if you're going to direct your child to pursue a scholarship, prioritize your son's education before anything else. Sports represent a tremendous and beneficial outlet, and will always play a prominent role in our country. But the one scholarship that anyone can qualify for, sans athletic ones, is an educational scholarship.

You may be saying to yourself that your son is not even able to read yet; however, if you're going to keep the scholarship dream alive, stay attuned to his cognitive interests. If he gravitates to science, take him to relevant fairs and museums to nurture that passion. Tune into TV programming or internet videos on how things are made, or watch series specials like "Earth" (which Discovery aired in the past).

The result may not be a college scholarship, but the process will make your son smarter and well-rounded.

# CHAPTER 90

# The Annual Home "Gift"

**W**hen you buy a home or a condo, I have a suggestion on how to improve the value of your home without detonating your savings plan: Once a year, plan to make one upgrade that improves the décor or curb appeal of your home. Consider this a birthday present for your residence. It can be as simple as replacing exterior lights or adding a ceiling fan on the porch. If your appliances are dated, replace one of them per year, and in five years your kitchen will add greater value to your home and net worth.

Even for those on tight budgets, this represents a small step to improve the appearance and feel of your home.

And if your annual project relates to landscaping, buy the tools you will need and do it yourself. It can be challenging, but such projects are very rewarding. And if done properly, they won't have to be repeated year after year. Plus, it's a free workout. Your yard will look better, and so will you.

# CHAPTER 91

# Home Improvement, or the Lack Thereof

If you own property, you likely know the costs associated with hiring professionals to perform repairs and maintenance. No one can afford to outsource every project. Small projects you try to fix yourself are the most vexing. That slow-dripping faucet, no matter what you do, won't stop running!

Calling in a handyman every single time a repair is needed will bankrupt you. Multiple repair jobs, coupled with regular maintenance (like mowing, shoveling, and general upkeep) can suck up all the free time you should be spending with your wife and son. And if those minor repairs really upset you, the stress can negatively affect the free time you do spend with your family.

Let me suggest one rule to consider, along with three steps, to make your life a little easier if you're a homeowner (or about to become one).

**The One-and-a-Half Rule:** Whatever repair you need to tackle, estimate the time it will take to do it. Be honest with yourself. Go for it, and if you give yourself an hour but you find you haven't fixed it in an hour and a half, it's time to call in a professional. Move on, don't consider it a failure, and admit you're not an expert at everything.

If you need to console your frustrations, remind yourself that you're an expert at your day job, which is helping to afford your home in the first place. If you're a stay-at-home dad, you're a professional parent and have the most important job life can bestow upon you.

So here are three things you can do to ensure you're maximizing your free time to tackle repairs when they come up:

1. *Reassess the family budget.* Find some areas where you can cut back in order to hire landscaping services, snow removal, or other time-consuming tasks. Designate that money to afford you time to spend with family.

2. *Cut the project in half.* Need to paint several rooms or work on landscaping jobs (like planting shrubs, trees, and perennial plants)? Paint half the rooms yourself and hire a painter to tackle the rest. For landscaping, hire someone to clear the area and deliver the plants, then plant them with help from your spouse.

3. *Schedule blocks of time with your family.* Designate two weekend blocks of time (e.g., Saturday morning and Sunday afternoon) for family time. The remainder of the weekend can be spent working on the home and property. Prioritize accordingly and skip projects you simply can't get to. If need be, spread a project over two weekends.

These suggestions will not only keep you sane, but will also ensure the money you earn is not wasted. And you won't neglect your number one job—being there for your son.

# CHAPTER 92

# The Family Nest: Wants versus Needs

**A**frenzy of activity takes place right before a child enters the world. It's referred to as "nesting," and it relates to parents trying to do everything they can to prepare a home for a newborn. You may have gone through this phase, but it goes on for years as your child progresses from crawling to walking to sprinting from one room to the next. You'll find babyproofing accelerates when Junior starts to walk and fragile items get moved to higher ground.

Inevitably, parents want to continue upgrading their homes. When discussions broaden to include a new kitchen, a man cave, or a professionally landscaped backyard, it's time to tap the brakes. Rome wasn't built in a day and, let's face it, you've got a long way to go before your home is featured in *Architectural Digest*.

Some projects are obvious and immediate, like a broken water heater. Others may reflect the simple desire to improve your home's décor. You have to separate wants from needs to avoid getting in over your head with serious credit card bills.

This lesson often gets lost in the frenzy of parenting, but it helps to put things in perspective. Referring back to the Bucket Strategy, you have more important priorities than building a music studio in your basement. Make sure you tackle the higher priorities first, like retirement or your son's college savings plan (529), before you delve into the things you want to do with your home.

Some projects are cash-intensive—a kitchen remodel being number one in most cases. Open a separate savings account and start depositing bonus checks in there for a few years. A tax refund or a work bonus is a great source to start a kitchen fund.

Deciphering wants from needs will help keep you sane as you start to improve the family nest.

# CHAPTER 93

# The Big Splurge

**Y**ou want a second house, a second car, or to enroll your kid in a private school. Maybe you have relatives in Italy and you've dreamed of an extended vacation to introduce your son or daughter to your family's heritage. Perhaps you're a teacher and you are off during the summer months, so you want to journey to South America for two months and hike the grueling Machu Picchu trail with your family.

Awesome! You have a long-term goal, which keeps you balanced and hopeful when you're changing diapers at 3:00 a.m. But you have no idea how you get from point A to B, financially.

I advise you to watch the movie *Lawrence of Arabia*, a twentieth-century masterpiece in which you will hear the catchphrase, "Nothing is written."

In other words, you can do anything. Set the goal, write it down, and go for it. Do the math and set a course:

1. Determine how many years you plan to execute on the goal.
2. Multiply the total years by twelve months.
3. Figure out the budget, soup-to-nuts (e.g., airfare, lodging, food, etc.).
4. Multiply that figure to account for inflation.
5. Divide that dollar figure by the total number of months you have to save for it.

Have some fun with this. Trust me, it's better than watching reruns of *Friends*. See how much a second home would cost and assume you'd pay in cash. Figure out a two-month itinerary in Italy or South America for the places you will visit and the costs.

When you break it down, as I've advised in past chapters, it's likely attainable if you prepare for it. A $12,000 trip to Italy in seven years equates to the following:

- Trip to Italy in 2027: $14,330. (The higher number here accounts for inflation.)
- Total months to prepare: 84.
- Total money required to save per month: $171.

Feeling discouraged given all your other saving priorities? Revisit that itinerary; maybe you can save on lodging-related expenses. Sign up for a travel rewards card and start banking air miles. Check out sites like LonelyPlanet.com for tips to save money.

When you think you've got a game plan, hash it out with your wife. If it's an entirely new concept, you'll have the math figured out and a sound plan. It's better than bringing up the idea in a half-assed manner. Conversations that start with, "I have a cool idea I've fleshed out and I want to see what you think," is better than, "Wouldn't it be great if . . ."

Besides, "ifs" are for dreamers. Real dads make sh*t happen!

# PART 9

## Family and In-Law Relations

# CHAPTER 94

# Section Preview: Family and In-Law Relations

When you grow up in a single-parent household, you are not exposed to the dynamics of inter family relationships. This represented my upbringing, and, as a result, I developed a blind spot.

I was blessed to have married into a family that was both welcoming and, more importantly, patient. I did not fully appreciate their patience for several years until I learned how my shortcomings (and my relatives) affected others.

My interaction with in-laws before this was extremely limited. When my parents separated, my mother made efforts to keep me in touch with my father's parents—her in-laws. That connection remained in place until I was twelve years old. Even when my parents officially divorced when I turned nine, my mother remained committed to keeping the family bonds intact. Those fell apart when my father chose to stop paying child support, a topic that I touched on in the finances section. I give my mother credit for managing these circumstances and zero fault for when the relationships I had with my father's side of the family diminished.

What I do not give her credit for is how she managed her new relationship with her daughter-in-law. Rather than approach her son's marriage as a new beginning and the chance to expand the family, my mother chose to hunker down and challenge the status quo. From the time we began to make our wedding plans until my mother's death, she never embraced my wife as a member of *our* family. For reasons I'm still trying to understand, my mom constantly tried to one-up my wife. Whether it was refusing to join us for the fortieth birthday party my wife hosted for me (my mother wanted to host her own party) or making a holiday meal she knew my wife would dislike, her approach put me between a rock and a hard place. The net result was my wife and I found ourselves in therapy.

Our time in therapy was well spent. I learned the value of professing respect to all members of our family. When my mother's behavior continued unabated, I demanded she join me in therapy to discuss how we could repair our relationship; this put my wife on even ground with my mother. Some wounds healed, some did not, but I made an honest and wholehearted effort to keep the family intact.

Hence, I appreciated the patience my in-laws exuded toward me as they watched their daughter manage a challenging situation of a husband who came packaged with a mother who never embraced her. I somehow managed to keep the peace in the end when I became my mother's exclusive caretaker as she battled cancer, loving her until the end, while remaining a committed and loving husband to my wife.

The point of this section is to share the wisdom I've garnered over the years and provide you with advice you may not need in its entirety. But hopefully a chapter or two will ring a bell on your end, and perhaps my suggestions can help you manage inter-family circumstances with greater diplomacy.

# CHAPTER 95

# The Most Important Word When Managing the Family: Tolerance

Thomas Paine wrote one of the most important literary works as our nation was founded when he penned *Common Sense*. In the book, he espouses a value Americans would need to succeed as an independent country: tolerance.

Paine reasoned you don't have to like everyone, nor do you have to agree with your neighbors. If your point of view represents the opinion of the majority, you still have to respect an individual's opinion that contrasts with everyone else. Tolerance is the glue that keeps a democracy together.

The same is true for those in your family you do not agree with or particularly like. Barring outright obnoxious behavior your child should not be exposed to (including drug or alcohol abuse), you have to make an effort to accept family for who they are. It can be a hard pill to swallow, but people are not going to change based on the presence of your one-year-old crawling around on the floor.

When your child is two, keep her perspective in mind. If your uncle screams at the TV when the opposing team scores a touch-down, she will consider this to be normal behavior. You're a dad; do you want your kid acting like that? Give your uncle a ribbing, tease him by asking if he needs his diaper changed, and tell him he's acting like a child.

Then glance at your daughter, shake your head, and maybe she'll get the message. If your uncle doesn't get the message, pull him into another room during a commercial and tell him to chill out when he's around your impressionable child.

You have to tolerate those in your family who are not perfect role models, but doing so doesn't excuse you from trying to modify their behavior.

# CHAPTER 96

# The Basics of Managing the In-Laws

**G**randparents are going to want to spend quality time with their grandchild. It's the nature of families. If you include in-laws who divorced and remarried, then the list grows.

It is a fantastic time, but it also can expose some rifts between you and your wife. Maybe that mother-in-law of yours wants the best for her granddaughter, but she doesn't see how that's possible on your income. Maybe your dad has issues with your opinionated wife, or he and his new wife's visits from Florida are lasting longer than anticipated.

Sometimes these rifts turn into chasms, especially on three hours of sleep, the strain of a long commute, or the consistent honey-do list discussions when your daughter is taking a nap. Friction between family members can be trying, and you have to maintain perspective. The more love a child has (and the more people that truly care about her), the better.

I suggest two rules to keep in mind when you and your wife become parents and find yourselves dealing with your extended families.

**Rule 1: Maintain and keep a united front.**

You and your spouse best oversee your nuclear family's interests . . . period. Take the advice offered by your parents or in-laws for what it is—an opinion. You and your spouse make all final decisions, and only when you are both on the same page.

If you are outnumbered by your in-laws, delay a decision until you speak in private with your wife. If your wife sides with her parents, tell her it's time to revisit how you make decisions as a couple, not as a group. This can be a hard conversation, and it's best to have it before a child comes into the picture.

What's the alternative? Kowtowing to your father-in-law every time he shares some cockeyed suggestion? Ask your wife how she would feel if she were expected to do the same.

You can't make a stink over little things, but you and your wife must establish boundaries. This leads to the second rule.

**Rule 2: You're responsible for your relatives, and the same goes for her.**

When it comes to your in-laws, it is not your place to explain to them the decisions you and your wife make. That's her job.

If the two of you have made a decision you know will upset your own mom and/or dad, the onus is squarely on your shoulders to manage that conversation. When you make a decision that runs counter to your parents' advice, don't rely on your wife to relay that to them. They could end up resenting her and circle back to question you about it when your wife is not present.

And you can always rely on one key phrase that states unequivocally that you and your wife are a united front: "Because that's what we've decided is best for (insert your child's name here)."

You'll likely encourage your child's grandparents to share advice, and many times it will be well-timed and needed. More often than not, they share well-intended wisdom. Encourage this, but remember that it's more important for you and your wife to make the decisions for your immediate family.

Things can (and will) get heated at times, but if you and your spouse maintain a united front, you have something to fall back on when your parents and in laws press.

# CHAPTER 97

# Setting Boundaries with Family

**Y**ou pull toward your house at 6:30 on Friday evening, feeling relieved a brutal work week has come to an end. But then you notice your mother-in-law's car in the driveway.

She's popped in again, unexpected, unannounced, and probably brought another cake.

If boundaries are not set early in the parenting process, they will not exist by the time Junior turns one. The same thing can be said about your parents, so this is a two-lane road when it comes to family. Both sides of the family need to respect your boundaries.

As charming as your father may be, your wife would probably appreciate a heads-up, or maybe she'd like a say when it comes to hosting. Despite the fact your dad mentions he doesn't need to be catered to, the house is a mess, Junior is crapping his pants on the hour, and your stay-at-home wife hasn't had the chance to shower in two days.

Or maybe you just want to get your son to bed on time so you can zone out with your wife on the couch. That's called *downtime*; every parent deserves it, and scheduling wise, pop ins never occur at the right time.

Use the acknowledgment/empathy approach suggested in chapter 28: "We love having you over, but we're trying to better manage our schedules. Moving forward, let's put time on the calendar for get-togethers so we can enjoy our time with one another."

No rule states you are required to accommodate relatives whenever they want to swing by and pop in.

# CHAPTER 98

# Laying Down Your Terms: Handling Critical Decisions

The "my way or the highway" approach to arguments and confrontations more often than not results in having to apologize in the short term. That goes for either side of the argument. Very few take this approach because, oftentimes, this temperament is not conducive to marriage in the first place.

When it comes to children, couples and their respective family members will have opinions that differ in regards to what is best for the children/grandchildren. Each side thinks they have the child's best interest at heart, but in many cases, it comes down to control and wanting to have a bigger say when it comes to final decisions.

Trying to make a decision under duress where the result is a zero-sum game between you and your wife produces a loser in the equation. Most times, that scenario can be avoided.

The first step in deflating an argument relating to your child's best interests, and about which "side" is right, is to agree that more time is needed to make a decision. Time gives room for everyone to breathe. Embrace the approach and hash it out with your spouse with an open mind. More often than not, a third or alternative way will come to the surface.

You'll be surprised how positive the process can be, especially if you and your wife come up with the solution together.

# CHAPTER 99

# Learning to Say "No" to Parents and Friends

If you never learn how to say "No," you'll never be in control.

Perhaps you and your brother have a tradition of watching NFL on Sunday afternoons or have season tickets. Maybe your buddies have a favorite town bar and you're still on the email thread for Saturday night outings. Or your mom needs your help again like she always does when there's fresh mulch to spread over her garden beds.

If you agree to participate in all three of these scenarios, you're doing two things—cutting into time with your child and creating more responsibilities for your wife. Your time is a precious commodity, especially if you're not a stay-at-home dad.

Set boundaries for yourself, and you'll be a better parent for it. It's important to keep in touch with and see friends. Invite those who don't have kids over for dinner so they'll see you in action caring for your baby girl, serving a meal, and putting her to bed. You can also invite friends over after the little one goes to sleep for beers in the backyard.

It's harder to say no to parents and in-laws, and there's not a single response for any given circumstance, but always use diplomacy and empathy. First, acknowledge their needs; second, note the motivation behind your decision.

"I'd love to lend a hand, but I'm giving my wife the break she deserves this weekend."

It doesn't leave much open to interpretation, which is the whole point.

# CHAPTER 100

# The Single Mom/Only Child Complex

**A** business meeting I had back in the early 2000s resulted in one of the most unusual conversations I ever experienced.

The client, a middle-aged woman married for twenty-plus years, asked about my pending nuptials (as she knew I was engaged). During our conversation, I shared that I was an only child and raised by a single mother. Upon hearing this, she shook her head.

"This is the exact same scenario my husband and I went through when I married him."

Her tone surprised me.

"Let me tell you something. Your wife? I hate to tell you, but she will never measure up to your mom's expectations. I speak from personal experience."

I felt completely off guard and had no idea what she was talking about. This conversation, which became very personal, completely digressed from the business we should have been discussing. But given the subject matter, I think she needed to speak about it as much as I needed to hear it.

I gave her the floor to speak her mind without interruption. In hindsight, this was one of the smartest things I ever did, for she spoke of an interesting quagmire that can surface between an only child and his mother.

No matter what your mother, distant relatives, or your wife tells you, the relationship you have with your mom went through a serious metamorphosis when you got married. The woman in your past (your mom) no longer represents your future. Your wife does. You may find yourself pulled in one direction by your mother and another by your wife. Your mom may question your loyalty when you decide not to spend a holiday with your side of the family. Once these types of conversations occur, they may become a source of anxiety for you because you know you may disappoint your mom again during the holiday season.

Know that you can manage the situation, though it may be delicate and require considerable diplomatic skills. The bottom line, however, is that your mother needs to accept new circumstances, respect you and your spouse's decision process, and embrace an important new member of the family—namely, your wife.

Here's some advice to help manage the situation if it relates to you:

*Your marriage demands respect.* Your marriage comes first and your child's best interests come next, and keeping a united front with your wife is paramount. Don't let your mother become a wedge between you and your spouse.

*Promote equality.* Hopefully you're active and participating in the life of your child. Plus, you're doing your part and helping around the house to take some of the burden off your wife. Your spouse is likely giving the same effort, if not more. In conversations with your mom, make note of everything your wife does for the baby, the household, and you. Ensure your mom understands how important your wife is to you, how terrific a mother she is, and how much you love her.

*Extend olive branches.* Haven't had your mom over for a few weeks? Are you due to invite her over for a Sunday brunch to provide quality time with your child? Let your wife extend the invitation. It's a savvy, diplomatic move. Reciprocate the same process with your wife's parents.

*Speak up.* If your mom becomes upset when her advice is not taken, or a particular tradition does not meet her expectations, have a blunt conversation with her. Convey to her your limits. The result of that chat has to be centered on your mother understanding your limits, how you and your wife make decisions, and how the two of you—and not grandma—are raising *your* child.

It can be a tough road, but letting things fester or putting your mom's needs and opinions before your wife's and child's will always result in a negative outcome for you. You'll be stuck in the middle, fighting a two-front battle.

Your mother was strong enough to raise a sensible and responsible child into a man. Don't be afraid to treat her as an equal adult.

# CHAPTER 101

# The Father-in-Law's Legacy

**H**ere's something many of us may be unaccustomed to in our family lives: a regular father figure. But now you find yourself with someone filling that role, namely, your father-in-law. He's older than you, filled with wisdom, and hopefully you and he formed a solid relationship. Only you can say if that's true, and every relationship is different. You married his daughter. That alone is an accomplishment. Ask any man with a teenage girl how he feels about his daughter dating boys, and you'll always find some level of resistance.

A father represents a role model and sets important expectations in the mind of a young girl, like the foundation of what, as a woman, she will expect from a man. The same is true in the reciprocal scenario. A mother sets the example for a man's future spouse.

I asked my wife, "What did your father mean to you in your family?"

Her answer: "He was always a constant. I knew he would always be there. The relationship he shared with my mother was always solid. I never doubted he loved my mother. He wasn't perfect. He was not always there emotionally for me, but I knew, in the end, I could count on him. Our whole family did."

That, my friends, is the definition of a legacy father. He made a positive impact. Thus, despite whatever shortcomings your father-in-law may have, if he's played a consistent and caring role in his daughter's life, he manned up and was a true father.

That's a great goal to set for yourself. And fortunately, you don't have to be a superhero or rich to attain that goal.

# CHAPTER 102

# Being Judged and Judging Brothers- and Sisters-in-Law

Hopefully you get along well with everyone on the opposite side of the family, and your side of the family treats your wife with respect and kindness. Sometimes feelings get hurt or bitter feelings arise if one sibling was mistreated during their childhood. As adults, tensions can sometimes linger. This can happen on both sides of the family. More often than not, it's resolved and people move forward.

When your son enters the picture, the rule of thumb should be that siblings on both sides of the family put their differences aside for the good of everyone. Whatever concerns you have about your older sister or your wife's lingering issues with her younger brother, you and your spouse have to agree to start with a clean slate. It's not about how you were wronged as a child; it's now about how everyone in the family appreciates and respects you and your wife as new parents. It benefits everyone when aunts and uncles are involved in the life of your son. The family bonds he forms with others in the clan will help him as he develops. Nothing is more valuable than longstanding relationships with family relatives.

So invite them to visit, and when they come, treat them like welcomed guests every time. Make an effort to travel and see them so they feel part of a new and growing family. Leave nothing to chance, and make sure you table any resentment you have toward anyone within your generation. It can be hard to start anew and leave the past behind, but you have to make a diplomatic effort for the benefit of your son.

Consider it a fresh start. You may find a new side to an in-law you never witnessed before. If they do something positive, acknowledge it. And make sure your wife knows you did so—she'll appreciate the effort you made.

# CHAPTER 103

# Drunk Uncle

If you've seen the *Saturday Night Live* skit, you recognize the reference of this chapter's title. It's the relative in the family who makes an idiot out of himself, or perhaps has a loud mouth. He (or she) has serious quirks, and they may drive you crazy. But guess what? He/She is family, so you have to deal with him/her.

Whether this person hails from your side of the family or hers, here's my advice: Take the high road and set a time limit. You may have no choice when it comes to sharing a house with a deadbeat, mooching brother-in-law who calls you "Gimpy" for reasons unbeknownst to you. For the sake of your marriage and children, you simply have to deal with it. As your kids get older, you'll figure out a way to manage him, or you'll simply turn the other cheek if he's outrageous. You can tell your kids it is the nature of family life, that you choose your friends, not your family.

What you don't have to agree to is spending an entire week with the man who calls you "Gimpy." Set a time limit if you're consistently irritated. For example, on a Thanksgiving weekend with your wife's family, take two cars, show up on Thanksgiving morning, and leave on Saturday. If your wife wants to stay longer (and with Junior in tow), why ruffle her feathers? Let her enjoy time with her family. Tell your in-laws you have plans to see a relative who's in town, or you have a friend who's relocating shortly. Make a polite excuse, and, if possible, make it the truth.

And if your wife expects you to spend every single holiday with the brother who calls you "Gimpy," then she must try to course correct his behavior. No one in a marriage should ever feel obliged to spend every single holiday with an obnoxious relative.

If that brother, or drunk uncle, is on your side of the family, provide your wife with the same means to excuse herself. Then make sure your obnoxious relative gets an earful for acting like a meathead around your child.

## CHAPTER 104
# Holidays with Family: Tip #1

**T**is the season to be annoying! Fa la la la la . . .

You steer your car into your father-in-law's driveway, but there's no room to park. You reverse and park on the street.

It was a two-hour car drive, and for half of it, your kid was crying. That soothing, calming baby music did nothing to improve the situation.

You park the car next to five others and your caffeine-infused glare rests on the house you are about to enter.

"Get the gifts and luggage. I'll get the baby," says your wife.

That translates into four trips back and forth to the car. Then you hear a loud shriek from your daughter. Your brain is screaming for earplugs.

Your in-laws are decent people. They are hardworking, committed to family, and respect you. The rest of your wife's family do not fit into the same category. You still haven't figured out how your awesome wife is genetically related to these people.

Halfway through the holiday meal, you realize just how "unique" your in-laws are after observing them. The three glasses of wine you consumed start to work against you when you ask your wife if she was adopted.

"Shut up," she snaps.

You have to carry on, period. This is the burden of tying the knot—you not only married your wife, you also married her family.

Spending an evening or a full day with the opposite side of the family is protocol during the holidays, but if the situation is this bad, I pose a solution. Focus on the kids in the family and play with them, or find someone who shares a hobby or interest of yours and dive deep on the subject if you must. You have to respect the time your wife has with her family just as much as she owes you the same courtesy.

Here's one family-relations rule to set for yourself: If the situation is challenging, you should not feel obligated to spend more than two full days with your wife's side of the family.

If you are tearing your hair out, set a boundary with your wife. You're willing to commit to two days, otherwise, you're pulling the ripcord and heading home early. If that means taking two cars, so be it. This will allow you to provide your wife and baby quality time with her immediate relatives while you protect yourself from entering a state of psychosis.

Flying long-distance? Read on.

# CHAPTER 105

# Holidays with Family: Tip #2

**R**udolph, with your nose so bright, guide me away from this awful fright!

"Sir, we're disembarking . . . Now."

You turn to face her with a soiled diaper in your hand, yet you refrain from throwing it at the impatient flight attendant. After all, hurling a diaper filled with crap at a high-altitude waitress after a four-hour flight would not end well.

Upon disembarking from said flight, you greet your in-laws, who will be hosting your immediate family for a five-day visit. They are wonderful in every respect, almost too much for your cynical nature to endure. Just once you'd love to hear your mother-in-law toss her manners out the window and bark out the F-bomb. There's got to be one in her somewhere, right?

On long-term visits, breaks are crucial. There's absolutely nothing wrong with taking an hour-long drive to give yourself some space. Ask your relatives to watch your son so you and your wife can get a break. Take your wife out to a nice dinner and movie. If it's a longer-than-average holiday visit, build in a window of time for a reprieve. If this requires a rental car, so be it.

During a long-term holiday stay with the in-laws, don't let circumstances or your wife dictate every moment. Make sure you have a say when the agenda is set.

# CHAPTER 106

# Holidays with Family: Tip #3

*I*t's beginning to look a lot like a nightmare!

Traffic got you to the first house on the list an hour late. Your mom hosted the first Christmas celebration (and her cooking was extraordinary, as usual), but then Junior spat up on schedule like Old Faithful and you needed a Starbucks double espresso to help keep you going. Now it's time to leave so you can make it on time for your in-laws' Christmas celebration, where ten people are awaiting your arrival.

You're already checking your watch. "Honey, we may be a bit late for dinner at your parents' house."

"Not on my watch. You should have taken the interstate."

An hour later, your brain screams for a triple shot of espresso.

"Get the gifts and luggage. I'll get the baby," your wife says with an inflection of disappointment at your scheduling mishap.

You've driven for a total of three hours, you are stuffed from the first meal, and all you want is a glass of wine and a comfy bed. It begs the question: When you're trying to attend two holiday celebrations in one day, is any part of the experience actually enjoyable?

Stop trying to please everyone all the time. You physically cannot do it. It's not fair to your baby, to your marriage, or to you. And trying to please everyone will simply make you miserable.

Here's one rule to live by: **one family, one holiday.** Go to your parents' home for Thanksgiving, her parents' place for Christmas, and swap it around every other year if it makes sense. Split up the lesser holidays too.

If you get pushback from in-laws, follow the logic in the chapter titled "Your Marriage Is Your Institution." You and your spouse can set the rules.

You're the father in *your* immediate family. Act like one.

# CHAPTER 107

# The "Pace" of Life

If you're like millions of Americans who delayed having kids to start a career or travel the world, you're not unusual. But there's a side effect to that decision. Your parents are older as well when they become grandparents. There are no pauses in life when it comes to aging, and that may affect how your son interacts with his grandparents.

Hopefully they are healthy and have many years ahead of them to enjoy spending time with your son and all their grandchildren. You've likely witnessed the incredible bond that forms between these generations. It's remarkable to witness, and the more time your child can spend with grandparents, the better.

But one common denominator comes with older grandparents. Their pace slows down with age, and that pace may match your son's when he is first learning to walk. You may find yourself walking ahead of a grandparent and your son.

Let them enjoy these moments. Step back and give them space and time to interact, and don't rush things. If you find yourself growing impatient, pause and let them enjoy one another's company. If you're all walking from a parking lot to a restaurant, let them hold hands and go at their pace, pausing to observe and discover something new and exciting.

You'll end up discovering something about *their* relationship, and it's wonderful to witness.

# CHAPTER 108

# The Only-Child Caregiver

**W**hether you're delusional from a colicky baby, cringing with excitement about the forthcoming birth of your child, or excited your daughter is finally potty-trained, you have another generation to think about.

One of the least discussed subjects when it comes to parental advice is how to be a caregiver to your parents. This includes several touchy subjects, not the least of which is the ultimate demise of your mother and father. Fortunately, we're living longer and medical advancements have provided the means to prolong life.

When your child enters the world, if you are an only child and have one or both parents who will require care down the road, you need to understand your role, their responsibilities, and how to manage a tragedy when it occurs.

This has to be a priority, and given you're an only child, you represent the only source of caregiving if your mother or father becomes ill. If you haven't had this talk with them, do it now, regardless of how healthy your mom or dad may be at present.

I have listed six topics you need to address, and if it makes your parents feel uncomfortable, so be it. I've paired each piece of advice with the rationale for addressing these points sooner rather than later.

1. **The Executor of the Estate.** If it has not been authorized by legal documents, you should be named the executor of your parents' estate. This provides you with oversight of all relevant issues relating to your parents' ultimate

demise. This is a standard element in the process of creating a will or testament.

*Why you need this:* Who (if anyone) has been put in charge of your parents' finances and possessions after they're gone? If there is neither a will nor a testament, this represents a major concern. The state may take possession or hinder your ability to distribute and manage their property unless there's a legal document in place.

2. **Power of Attorney.** Without being granted power of attorney over your parents' finances, you have no legal right, or means, to access their money to pay for healthcare needs. According to the *Wall Street Journal*, this notarized document enables you to represent or act on behalf of a loved one.[1]

*Why you need this:* If your divorced mother suffers from a stroke and she cannot write a check or make payments for her care, who will cover the immediate expenses in a crisis? This could require you to dig into your personal savings account.

3. **Life Support Issues.** If a legal document (called a living will or an advance directive) is not in place providing you the right to cease and desist life support, you have no legal grounds to terminate what could be a hopeless situation. It's scary to think about, but it is the reality of being an only child, and this burden should fall on you, not someone outside the family.

---

1   Power, William. "The Difficult, Delicate, Untangling of Our Parents' Financial Lives." *Wall Street Journal*. March 27, 2016. https://www. wsj.com/articles/the-difficult-delicate-untangling-of-our-parents -financial-lives-1459130770.

*Why you need this:* You need this legal document to authorize you to make the final decision if and when your parents face long odds of recovering on life support. Otherwise the state or medical professionals caring for your parent may have an equal, if not greater, say with you.

4. **Wealth/Healthcare.** Medicare or Medicaid alone will not pay for your parents' healthcare needs, nor the medications they will be required to take as they age. How do they plan to cover these costs? If they are relying on a pension to fund these expenses, is that pension at risk? If so, what happens if that source of income disappears?

*Why you need this:* During the Great Recession, many companies outsourced their pension obligations and management to third-party companies. These spin-off subsidiaries claimed bankruptcy, and, under Chapter 11 laws, individuals with pension claims saw massive reductions in entitlements. You have no guarantee your mom or dad's pension is 100 percent secure; therefore, a contingency plan should be in place, such as downsizing one's home or investigating financial products like annuities that assure an income for life.

More importantly, you need a bird's-eye perspective about your parents' nest egg and how they plan to fund their long-term retirement needs.

5. **The Mortgage.** Is your mom and/or dad's house almost paid off? Have they lived there for decades? How much do they owe? Their property not only represents an important nest egg, their mortgage affects their cash flow. If they do owe a sizable amount to the bank and have

an adjustable-rate mortgage (ARM), what happens if mortgage rates jump? Mortgage ARM rates are tied to increases in the federal government's prime rate.

*Why you need this:* You may discover there is no nest egg, and that your parents own little, if any, percentage of their home. Perhaps they took out a home equity line to finance your college tuition and never got around to paying it off. That debt may translate into the loss of their home in a crisis. Reciprocally, you can use the home as a source of immediate financing if health costs spike in the short term, via a home equity line of credit (HELOC). If you have power of attorney, you can make that decision.

6. **Paperwork.** The final element to note is the need to have all these documents accounted for and placed in a location that is easy to access. It could be a home safe, a security deposit box, or simply a well-known place in the house. You should be able to access any and all documents in case of an emergency—and make sure they are kept in a fireproof box.

*Why this is just as important:* No one plans a heart attack, a disabling fall, or an accident—it just happens. Not knowing where to find critical paperwork when a crisis arises will only complicate matters when it falls upon you. If your mom or dad live a thousand miles away, quick access to paperwork in an emergency is critical.

Given you're an only child or the oldest of your siblings, your parents are on the hook to ensure they are not leaving behind a mess for you to sort out after they have passed away. Address these issues with them before any serious medical circumstances arise to avoid unnecessary chaos.

# CHAPTER 109

# The Wisdom of Outsiders

**P**ut your parents, in-laws, and all of your relatives to the side for a moment. They will speak volumes and share bits of wisdom along the way. Let's now consider advice provided by people *outside* your family.

It may be a nanny on the playground or a friend with four kids. Some guys will feel offended at being told how to manage their kids or a particular circumstance, and they will be turned off since they have an ego and think they know best about how to approach certain situations or challenges. If you are one of these guys who think they can tackle any and all problems on your own, I have some healthy advice for you to consider: Listen. Be polite. Don't object right away, and think about the suggestion for a few days. If you're a man who is now a father but did not have a male role model as you grew up, it doesn't hurt to keep an open mind to the advice you receive.

Give someone the floor to speak. Don't cut them off. You can always disregard the advice, but if it results in you becoming a better parent, isn't that a better outcome?

More often than not, these advice-givers simply care about your child. Put your ego aside and explore why they came to a particular conclusion.

## CHAPTER 110
# Righting the Ship

**A** moment comes, early in one's days as a new father, when the past comes back to bite you on the rear end. It relates to your family, long-lost friends, and connections you made before becoming a father, and it leaves an unsettling taste in your mouth. Perhaps there's unfinished business or a relationship you once shared with someone that went dormant for unexplained reasons.

It could be an estranged relative or cousin (perhaps someone you spent your childhood with at a family summer home), a person who influenced you during high school or college, a respected teacher, or an old roommate. Sometimes thoughts of this person can come at you like a light in the dark—*What happened to them? Where are they in the world?*

It happens simply because you've entered a major life stage, and curiosity gets the better of you. You wonder if perhaps they are up at 3:00 a.m., like you, feeding their kid or looking forward to a day with their grandchildren.

Take advantage of this. Reach out to them, reconnect, and share what's happening in your life. In 99 percent of the cases, they'll be happy to hear from you.

If there's a grudge of some kind, or you feel slighted by a person who made a positive impact on your life, why not try to settle things and reestablish a relationship with them?

For those of us who come from divorced families and lost touch with relatives on our father's side of the family, this is a terrific moment in your life to reconnect. If nothing else, it's worth the effort for your own satisfaction. You may rekindle a connection that truly meant something to you in the past, and, moving forward, perhaps that individual's perspective can make you a better father.

Maybe you can spend vacation time with that long-lost cousin who has a child of his/her own now. How awesome would that be?

# PART 10

## Role Models and Your Community

# CHAPTER 111

# Section Preview: Role Models and Your Community

While growing up in Ho-Ho-Kus, New Jersey, several institutions played a bigger role in my life than one would expect.

The Boy Scouts of America provided me with two experiences—the opportunity to be surrounded by male role models and the lessons that came with being held accountable and responsible. Both elements were absent on some level thanks to not having a father involved in my life, and I cherish my experience with the Boy Scouts. I can't say it made a man out of me, but when you participate in three-day canoe treks and hikes with a dozen others, you need to be dependable and develop loads of stamina. You can't take shortcuts if the troop is relying on you to collect firewood or cook. In these kinds of circumstances, children and adults alike are *counting* on you.

The Boy Scouts also exposed me to other fathers and adult troop leaders in a setting I was unused to. Rather than seeing them as coaches or sideline parents at sporting events, we were in the bush, literally. I had the opportunity to get to know these men and observe them as they exuded leadership and warmth to the kids, dispensed fatherly advice, and contributed necessary manpower. I looked up to them and appreciated their time and patience, especially with smart aleck scouts who always pushed the limits. Namely, me.

Out in the bush, they held greater authority than in our suburban surroundings, and when I needed to be disciplined, I got the message. I clearly remember one father's response to me when I forgot to take care of an important task for the troop during a two-week camp outing in upstate New York. His reaction was short, cold, and disheartening. "Well, Kendall, I'm really disappointed."

He then turned and just walked away. I'll never forget it. I realized my role in the troop and place among the other scouts was of equal importance with everyone else. My goal thereafter was not to let him or another troop leader down again. When you come from a home where the only voice of discontent comes from one's mother, it hits a little harder when you let someone else's father down in the middle of the forest.

The Boy Scouts, as an institution, continues to face one scandal after another. The same is true, on a much broader (and scarier) level, with religious institutions. It seems every major institution we counted on during our youth has been hit with reports of abuse, mismanagement, or corruption.

So . . . be selective when you choose community institutions for your son or daughter to be involved with, and then volunteer to participate. Don't do drive-by drop-offs; go inside and get involved. If that results in something you are not comfortable or familiar with, be the man!

And if you find yourself completely out of your comfort zone (e.g., canoeing for hours in a swamp) be a leader. Take the reins and be a role model for everyone.

## CHAPTER 112
# Your Number One Role Model

**I**f you were predominantly or exclusively raised by a single mother, this chapter is centered on one undeniable fact: Your mother likely represents your number one role model.

She kept the house in order, put food on the table, and likely managed a schedule on par with a Fortune 500 CEO. If you had siblings in the house, multiply everything noted above by the number of brothers and sisters you have. It's impressive, right?

She was also the center of your world during the most critical years of your upbringing. Perhaps your mother's influence espoused the value of knowledge and education. The result is that you, at this very moment, are reading a book offering advice about how to be the best father you can be. That says something in itself; you want your child to have a better life than you did.

Take a moment and put yourself in a neutral frame of mind. Ask yourself what she did best. What are the most important things she did to help you get to where you are today? Did she keep you off the streets at night with sports programs? Did she provide you access to tutoring services when you struggled in school? What did she prioritize when you were growing up that had the greatest impact on your life?

Stay in this same frame of mind and ask what your mom could (or should) have done to be a better parent. You'll surely find a deficiency somewhere in your upbringing, you just have to be honest to identify it.

Perhaps you had a friend your mom thought was an angel, but

got you into a ton of trouble. Were you given little or no direction when it came to puberty and girls? Did your mother teach you the value of money, the importance of a work ethic, or how to treat women? Was there a gap somewhere in terms of knowledge, or a critical lesson you should have learned at an earlier age?

These aren't things to hold against your mom, but are questions that will help identify the values you will want to instill in your son to help him throughout his life.

After you drill down into this process, invite your mom out for a wonderful meal. Pick her favorite restaurant and thank her for everything she did for you. She truly was a miracle worker to parent you on her own, so share your appreciation.

Then ask her about those areas where you want to do a better job for your son. Be honest, because this is for your son's benefit. Listen to what she says and it may prove the most honest conversation you ever had with her. You'll have a better understanding of the challenges she faced as a parent, which will better prepare you for similar circumstances.

## CHAPTER 113
# Seek Out and Find Other Role Models

The last chapter focused on the woman who raised you and what she did right. If you dig deeper into your past, you will likely find other people who played a great role in your life as you grew up. They influenced you in a positive way and shaped the man you've become. Even if it was a brief relationship, and regardless of gender, who else helped to point you in the right direction?

The positive influences you had in your life as a child are worth replicating for your own. Once you identify friends and relatives who offer something special, a value worthy of passing along, introduce these "MVPs" to the next generation—your daughter.

It can be as simple as identifying someone in your family with a strong work ethic who works extra hard to provide for his/her family. It could be a close friend who continues to receive promotions at work, is a skilled craftsman, or an expert in a given field. How did they arrive at their place in the world? More likely than not, their success stemmed from hard work, and as your daughter matures, she should have that person in her orbit. He or she may provide a different and beneficial influence in addition to what you can pass along.

No man is an island, so make a point to build bridges to other people who can shape your daughter's view of the world in a positive light.

# CHAPTER 114

# Kind People Matter

**L**ife has introduced you to many types of people since your childhood: ambitious coworkers, dedicated first responders, and intelligent people with advanced degrees, like doctors and lawyers. They all serve a purpose in your community. Now that you are a father, there is one particular type of person worth noting that matters more than ever.

This is the person who is kind and cares about the well-being of your son. You may have overlooked these individuals during the days you were single or in college. But they've always been there—a friendly neighbor or an aunt you do not often get to see due to distance or circumstances.

These kind souls played a role in your life when you grew up, and they are wonderful people to involve with your family. They espouse compassion, understanding, patience, and the desire to care for others. Aren't those great qualities for your son to possess?

Make a point to involve these individuals in your family life, and if you're lucky, their values will be shared and appreciated by the next generation.

# CHAPTER 115

# Shunning Media Stereotypes: The Idiot Father

It started three decades ago with the introduction of Homer Simpson, or perhaps years before when Chevy Chase portrayed Clark Griswold in the movie *National Lampoon's Vacation*. The theme of the idiot father continues today in movies, TV series, and commercials. One recent commercial that aired during the 2016 summer Olympics showed a group of fathers trying to pole vault over a pool with a long pole. Their wives looked on from a distance with a mature and rational perspective, suggesting how they—compared to their husbands—are the adults in the scenario.

If you pay attention, you'll see how fathers in the media are often cast as buffoons and morons. We represent an easy target in the eyes of producers, directors, and creative media professionals. Traditional networks like ABC, NBC, and CBS (in particular) have a passion for positioning fathers as subservient members of the traditional American family. Media dads are portrayed essentially as adult children who go from one stupid decision to the next in an effort to generate a laugh.

Now that you're a father, do you want to associate yourself with this stereotype? Is this how you act in front of your daughter, or more importantly, do you want her to associate this stereotype with fatherhood?

If this theme comes up in a show your family is watching

together, turn the channel. If a corporation airs a commercial portraying the idiot father, don't buy their products. Go one step further and voice your displeasure via social media.

We are equals to our wives, and we should demand the same level of respect from companies or studios that want our business.

# CHAPTER 116

# "Optimism is a Force Multiplier"

**A**nother quote by none other than Colin Powell to keep in mind throughout your journey as a parent when you come across naysayers and doubters is "Optimism is a force multiplier."[1]

Those of us who grew up in divorced homes may voice our concerns or troubles in any number of situations. It begs the question—does negative energy help in any way? You likely come across these people in your office. Does it help or hurt overall productivity?

Everyone is allowed to be negative sometimes, but if you find people in your family, work life, or fellow parents are constantly sour, is that beneficial for your daughter? If you go along with that negative perspective, what example will you set for her?

When you find yourself on the dark side of matters, apply some optimism. If your daughter sees you suggesting how to make a bad situation better, or playing devil's advocate and being positive, it may trickle down into her outlook on life.

And when your wife, children, and immediate family feel uplifted by your point of view, it represents the "force multiplier" element, and it's infectious; you'll see people join in and help to turn the tide.

Besides, a person who comes across like the Debbie Downer

---

1    Powell, Colin. *My American Journey* (Ballantine Books, 2003).

character from *Saturday Night Live* isn't fun to be around.

Teach your daughter to always have hope and espouse the value of finding a better way forward.

## CHAPTER 117
# The Power of Wisdom

**W**e live in an age of limitless information. It is stunning how the past twenty years have empowered us with a wealth of knowledge through the web, online video, and sources like Wikipedia. One only has to tap the laptop keys to reveal answers to real-world challenges. Need instructions on how to reconfigure a baby's car seat? A YouTube search supplies 73,000 results.

What we do not have readily available is wisdom, which is defined as "the quality of having experience, knowledge, and good judgment."[2]

Finding sources that supply that valued combination of experience, knowledge, and good judgment are rare indeed, and you have to search for them as a father. More often than not, it comes from other parents you know and respect, regardless of gender. When you discover individuals who share your values, make a point to connect with them and build new friendships.

Parenthood demands greater wisdom as your child ages. If, in addition to your wife, you can find a half dozen good navigators during your journey as a parent, you'll be a better father for it.

---

2    *Oxford Languages*. Oxford University Press, 2020.

# CHAPTER 118

# Your Local Radar

When your daughter is one year old and no longer completely vulnerable like she was at one month, life begins to settle down. You start to find a rhythm in life that makes everything easier. Sleep and feeding times normalize, and you'll find your work life is more manageable because you're getting more sleep.

This is a good time to get your radar going in your neighborhood. It's time to assess where you live and work, and where the institutions are located in your hometown. Going day to day and keeping up with the challenges of being a new dad can take your eye off the long term implications of remaining where you currently reside and work.

It's worth thinking about the schools, the commute, and institutions you and your family will encounter when your little girl gets older.

Look at your block or building. Is this a great place to raise a child? How is the school district here? If your child has special needs or shows significant intelligence, does the school system have the means to accommodate her? You may not know what she needs, but will she be given the chance to excel?

What about your town? Does it represent a long or short commute for you? If and when you need a bigger car, is parking an SUV going to be harder on the streets in your neighborhood? Are there cultural institutions in town or close by that will help to enlighten your child?

Set your radar even further out on you and/or your wife's

careers. Are companies moving in to the area, or folding their tents and moving elsewhere? Are there good growth prospects that will enable you to provide for your family?

As in real estate, "location, location, location" matters when it comes to raising your daughter. Where you live represents the foundation of her life, and the first priority is to give her the best chances possible. Consider everything from your home, to the neighborhood, to your town. If you decide it's worth moving, set yourselves up for the long term.

Then check out the financially-related chapters in this book. They will provide some strategies for affording a move into a new home, neighborhood, or town that will best meet the needs of your family.

# CHAPTER 119

# New Kids, New Friends

**A** social dynamic unfolds when your child starts to walk. Soon enough, you start visiting playgrounds, exposing you to other parents and their children. Conversations start, children begin to play, and this process multiplies one weekend to the next.

As your child starts to socialize, you also have the opportunity to make new friends and extend your social network, which is an opportunity you should embrace wholeheartedly.

The friends you made since childhood, college, and at work often move to new towns or states, and it becomes less convenient to get together regularly, if at all. But the chance to meet new people and provide your daughter with playdates can fill the friendship gaps and provide relief when your family gets bored.

Make a call, invite some parents over, and order a pizza for everyone to enjoy. Or take it to the next level and enjoy a couple's night out with these new connections. You and your spouse will find yourself with a wider connection of new friends, and your child will have plenty of kids to play with.

# CHAPTER 120

# The Parenting/ Friendship Divide

The visit to a friend who is an hour's drive south didn't seem like a big deal before children, but coupled with nap times, feedings, and conflicting schedules, it makes things more complicated.

You will find that as your child passes the one-year mark, you'll start to meet other couples closer to home. You'll find people when you're walking around with your son in the stroller or pushing him in the swing at the playground. When your kid starts to interact with other children, another world opens up as you meet the parents of your son's new friends. A common bond connects parents to one another, for they face the same challenges and delights. So take advantage of the chance to broaden your pool of friendships.

This represents a unique time in life when your exposure to new people extends beyond childhood friends, college buddies, or work cohorts. You're living through a challenging time with a common bond that connects one parent to another. When there's an opportunity to broaden your pool of friendships, take advantage of it.

It's also great for your son. If he connects with a child on the playground and you get a dialogue going with another parent, ask to exchange phone numbers. When and if you get together, perhaps your wives will hit it off. The other benefit is you'll have four pairs of eyes watching the kids play.

Your circle of friends will start to grow closer to home, and your son will pick up some solid social skills.

You'll see your college roommate less often, but he/she is no less of a friend, and this is part of becoming a parent. Use the opportunity to broaden your network locally and you won't end up regretting the chance to see close friends on a more frequent basis.

# CHAPTER 121

# Broken Institutions and What to Do About Them

At no other point in American history have citizens been so cynical and suspicious of the institutions that represent the framework of our society.

A basic understanding of history could cite the assassination of John F. Kennedy or the Watergate scandal as the events that started to erode government credibility. The Great Recession worsened it, and it's hard to find other institutions that haven't been privy to mistrust. The Catholic Church raised alarms, Wall Street produced Bernie Madoff, and even the Boy Scouts of America were accused of discriminating against homosexuals.

It begs the question—what is the best strategy if a couple wants to involve their children with institutions that have recent histories of transgressions? Given the volume of legal and moral challenges that have taken place, is there any safe refuge free of scandal or corruption?

What makes this even more challenging is that we (and our parents) were involved and active during our childhoods with these same institutions. In most cases, these community institutions provided a rich experience, free of the moral and ethical challenges that exist today.

If you decide to move forward with a community organization whose reputation was tarnished, there are things a father (and mother) can do to utilize these resources and keep your child safe—stay active, get involved, and become a leader.

If those in charge welcome you and your family, be civil, ask a ton of questions, and start building rapport with other parents. Volunteer your time and offer your opinion whenever you can, and work to understand the politics of the organization. Don't be afraid to engage with those at higher levels. Set an example for your daughter and start playing an active role at events. Do what it takes to be recognized, and instill confidence in others that your primary goal is to provide a positive experience for everyone involved. In due time, you'll be a leader and have greater say.

This strategy will provide you with a bird's eye view of what's going on, greater access to the facts, and the chance to influence the overall process.

This may seem like overkill, but many of those who went along with the flow and exuded blind faith in organizations that should have acted properly got burned. The consequence was their children suffered.

If your heart tells you that your daughter will benefit from involvement with the institution in question, go for it. Use your head and leadership skills to ensure you're not kept at arm's length from how the organization conducts itself.

# CHAPTER 122

# Leadership and Showing Up

**W**oody Allen once said that 90 percent of life is simply showing up.[3] It's not a hard concept to understand, and it is especially true when it comes to kids. Staying engaged with their sport and hobby interests is the best way outside of the home to remain involved.

All you have to do is volunteer your time. And then . . . show up.

Parenting in the modern age is more complicated than when we were kids. We commute for longer periods of time, remain tethered to work through smartphones and laptops, and social media plays an active role in our lives (whether or not we want to admit it). What really counts, however, is sharing special time with your daughter and committing yourself to stay involved.

Making your interests and experience known to organizations will provide more opportunities than you can possibly imagine. There are never enough parent volunteers when it comes to group activities, so deal yourself into the game.

If you can bring a basic knowledge of a sport or hobby, provide leadership and get involved. You don't have to be a star athlete to teach the basics. Given how many youth programs are oriented around sports, you can also do your homework. Infinite online resources can help flesh out a training program for newbies to

---

3    Braudy, Susan. "He's Woody Allen's Not-So-Silent Partner." *New York Times*, August 21, 1977.

any given sport. Prepare in advance, come with a game plan if you're the coach, and you'll find the rewards for involving yourself far outweigh the time you could spend doing something with your child alone.

You'll also be able to put a lid on parents who get out of line. That alone is something to look forward to. Otherwise, you're just another parent on the sideline.

# CHAPTER 123

# The First Rule of Social Media

**Y**ou've likely viewed hundreds of pictures of babies posted on social media. Once a couple has a child, the volume of a couple's posts turns stratospheric. You will likely get caught up in it. Parents start feeding on one another's posts about child development, the "firsts" (first poop, first steps, etc.), and the simple love affair that blossoms when a child comes into the picture.

At some point, you'll find yourself posting your fourth pic of the week and going back several times to see who responded. This represents twenty-first century human behavior, and it's here to stay.

When you find yourself spending more than fifteen minutes a day logging into social sites, it's time to tap the brakes. It may be a casual visit (or twenty) during a lazy day at the office, or perhaps it's during a holiday when you're shocked to see your daughter's elf costume has only received twenty likes when it deserves fifty.

Add all that time up and then, before you know it, you're spending two to three hours a week of your life on Facebook.

Here's the suggestion: Replace those digital Facebook "connections" with real ones. Limit your posts to a handful per week, but at the same time, set up playdates, reconnect with old college friends, and reach out to set up face-to-face gatherings. Use that lazy day in the office to email a friend you've lost touch with. Set up a lunch get-together during the week with a colleague who has children around the same age. Share stories and a meal with extended family or neighbors. And if a playdate happens during the summer, crank up the grill and throw back a beer or two.

If digital socializing takes time away from your chance to interact with real people, you end up missing the opportunity to connect with friends and family.

If a picture speaks a thousand words, a great afternoon with friends equates with a meaningful chapter. Those chapters will end up making a great novel later in life when you recall the early days of your fatherhood experience.

# CHAPTER 124
# The Second Rule of Social Media

If the first rule is about time management, the second can be defined as reputation management. The minute you start griping about kids, work, or your struggles as a parent, you devalue your worth as a role model.

It's pretty straightforward. You're a parent working to raise a promising young girl or boy. Sleep deprivation, working long hours, diaper duty, or complaining about the terrible twos debases the overall effort you are making. When your friends and family see a post highlighting the negative aspects of parenting, it puts a spotlight on what you do not enjoy about being a dad.

Is it worth it?

Consider one solution: State the facts, free of adjectives or negative insinuations, and make it as deadpan as possible. Self-deprecation works well. If you feel the need for empathy, you'll likely receive some compassionate responses. And it may even make you feel better about the challenges you're experiencing.

Or . . . man up and stop whining on social media. Let lesser men who aren't as strong show how weak they truly are.

PART 11

Guest Interview #3

# CHAPTER 125

# Mark and Steve—Two Dads and Gay Parenting

**M**ark and Steve are two dads raising three wonderful children in Bergen County, New Jersey. Their mutual path to fatherhood represents an area of considerable interest within the gay community: adoption and gestational surrogacy.

Mark hails from a town outside Montreal, and, prior to becoming a stay-at-home dad, he had a successful career within the retail and visual merchandising field.

Steve started his career in investment banking before segueing into management consulting and digital media, then returning to investment banking. Today he works as a financial advisor to a broad range of public and private sector clients. He's a New Yorker, raised in the suburbs of Long Island.

Mark and Steve have been together for seventeen years and were officially married in 2012 after same-sex marriage was legalized in New York. The Supreme Court ruled in favor of gay marriage shortly thereafter, a critical turning point in our nation's history. The result broadened the definition of the word "family" itself, and it's worth exploring Mark and Steve's story to understand how our communities are adapting and growing.

They became official parents when their son was born in February 2013. Twins followed in February 2016, and the five of them now reside in the suburbs outside New York City.

Here's their story.

KENDALL: Please assume I'm totally naïve and share with us how a gay couple go about having biological children.

STEVE: The only way to do it is through a surrogacy, and gestational surrogacy . . . means that you have an egg donor who provides that component of the genetic material and the egg is fertilized.

A big misconception that people have is the surrogate, the woman [who] carries the baby, is also the genetic parent. That's not the case. That's called traditional surrogacy. But that's generally not done anymore. It creates a lot of emotional and other issues if the woman who's carrying the baby is also the genetic mother.

[You] have a separate egg donor . . . [you] go to a fertility clinic and you find your egg donor, and then you fertilize the eggs. Then they get transferred to a gestational surrogate, who gets pregnant like any other person.

KENDALL: When the two of you were starting a relationship, was having kids a top priority and a given?

STEVE: It's funny, we talked about it very early and then we really didn't pursue it. We were younger . . . and we were pursing our life and careers. Traveling and things like that. As we got older, we needed to decide if we wanted to do this. We decided that we were going to make the commitment to do it.

MARK: It was pretty quick. We decided to move forward, and it happened more quickly than we anticipated.

KENDALL: Regarding gay parenting and the community at large, what are some of the challenges gay couples have that heterosexual couples do not have that are less obvious?

STEVE: I don't know whether this is obvious or not, but . . . acceptance. I worry about our kids being accepted because sometimes kids don't understand there are different kinds of families.

MARK: Some people feel bad sometimes when they come to me [and] say, "What does your wife do?"

STEVE: Even though it's obvious. But something that I think we wonder about, maybe it's our own insecurity but . . . is there something lacking because there's not a mother figure? I don't know.

KENDALL: Your point about being two dads, believing it is obvious, however, that's something we never would think about in the straight community.

STEVE: Well, we always have to come out. There's always the assumption that there is a mother, so until people get to know us, we have to explain that we are a two dad family.

MARK: I get insecure [of] the reaction I get when I meet new parents, or they're the people from school, and you get a certain face. That makes me uncomfortable. Sometimes they are positive, but sometimes . . .

STEVE: Not always.

MARK: But sometimes I feel like I just turned these people off. There's always that.

STEVE: Sometimes they're surprised. Sometimes they want to show you how accepting they are, so they—

KENDALL: They go overboard?

STEVE: They over go overboard. We get some people who are like, "Oh! I wasn't expecting that," and they need to digest it.

KENDALL: Your family resided in New York City and then, more recently, in the suburbs of Bergen County, New Jersey. What were you most attuned to, or looking for, that made your home town appealing?

STEVE: I think we were looking for a place that felt a little bit more on the progressive side. Our town is that. We wanted a place with good schools . . . I think we share a lot of similarities that other couples have in that regard.

MARK: And we did see a couple rainbow flags on the houses.

STEVE: Yeah.

KENDALL: Did you really?

MARK: We saw a few. We thought that was interesting.

STEVE: We didn't have a strong connection here, but we heard really good things about Bergen County. We spent time touring around the town and the people, and liked it.

MARK: It's the best decision we ever made so far.

KENDALL: Awesome. What should gay couples keep in mind when choosing a new place to live when you have kids?

MARK: Something that makes them comfortable.

STEVE: I think you should make sure you feel comfortable in the town. I think that it's difficult to pinpoint—you want something that reflects your values. For us, diversity, inclusion, and people who reflect those values are important. You need to read about a town. You need to read about a community and talk to people. Open mindedness. Some places . . . may be harder, but at least go there understanding what the challenges might be.

Our kids have been really accepted. I do think about how kids become more aware as they get older, how our oldest will be in fifth grade, or in middle school. Things like that. We think we picked a place where people are open minded and accepting. I think that's important.

MARK: We also want to blend in with the people and just live our life, and connect with everybody on the same level.

KENDALL: Did you experience any concerns from others during your home search?

STEVE: A lot of people were surprised we wanted to leave New York City because they felt like the city had more diversity and was more progressive. We actually lived in Harlem before. It's funny, we were a minority. We loved it. Our son had lots of friends at the park who were African American. It was very progressive.

[But] it was important for us to have more space, things that a lot of straight families want. We wanted to have a good education system and things like that.

I think some were just like, "Really? You want to go to the suburbs? A white, heterosexual place?" That was a little bit of my concern. Were we going to lose our connection to the gay culture?

MARK: For me, being a stay-at-home dad, if we had to take the subway with three kids every day to go to school, it would be painful. I just want to get out and drive my minivan and have more liberty with three kids.

KENDALL: It's a quality of life issue then.

MARK: It was. Also, we lived in New York City. We paid for prime. You [could] go to a Broadway show, but we didn't do that. We just didn't benefit from all of that.

STEVE: We had a lot of different friends, but once you have a kid, you try to focus on kids. Once we moved here, we're not as connected with our friends in the city. It's just a difference. It's a choice. Now we connect with other people.

KENDALL: Has your older son encountered any questions about having two dads? And what about other moms and dads you've run into? What's the response been?

MARK: Actually, the one that's teaching all the people is our son. He is telling everyone, "Hey, I have two dads," and he's excited about it. His friends are four years old, and they are so much more advanced.

STEVE: That's the amazing thing. Kids—they learn prejudice. They learn bias. He doesn't know any difference, so he freely, innocently, will say, "Papa and Daddy" at the playground. It makes me really happy. I hope it stays the same.

I connect with a lot of other gay dads. I think that's a fear that a lot of us have, because they become more self-aware. That's where the challenge is in society. You want to build kids with good, strong character. I hope we're developing him with that character [so] that he continues to feel proud of his family. But, right now, it's—

MARK: It's so cute.

STEVE: He knows no difference. He knows people have moms, but he knows that he has two dads, and he's totally fine with that.

KENDALL: For gay men or women who are worried about starting a family, what's your advice to them regarding fertility, choices, and the process? What's a key thing for them to bear in mind?

STEVE: It depends. We actually had thought about adoption, and then we thought about international adoption. We . . . started exploring adopting a child from Vietnam or Guatemala. Then the treaties in those countries ended, where they banned gay adoption.

KENDALL: Interesting.

STEVE: That was originally the path we were going down. Vietnam and Guatemala were allowing single men to adopt. Nobody allowed gay couples. A lot of [gay] men pretend that you're single to adopt. We had thought about domestic adoption too, then that got derailed. There were a whole bunch of scandals. Then we decided, "Why shouldn't we have a kid of our own?"

The issue with surrogacy is it's very expensive. I'm totally grateful, but it's sad that a lot of people can't do it because of the money. That's a hard reality. I have a recent friend that did a foster to adopt, so it didn't cost them anything. They are in Maine. They fostered a kid. He was three or four years old, and they just completed the adoption. He seems like the most amazing kid. There's a lot of ways if money is prohibitive and you're willing to go down the foster-to-adopt route, so there are options. If you really want to become a dad, you can become a dad.

KENDALL: This is a little more personal, but regarding your families, what was the moment like when you shared the news that you were expecting?

MARK: Because it's such a big process, they already knew that we were in the process, so they were all in it with us. They were waiting to see when we picked a surrogate.

STEVE: We shared everything with them. We shared egg donor profiles, surrogate profiles. We involved our families in the process.

MARK: The only people that didn't know were our friends.

STEVE: Yeah, we kept it from friends.

MARK: Until we knew we were very far along the way.

STEVE: Kind of like straight people do.

KENDALL: They wait until the end of the first trimester.

MARK: But the family was very involved. There's so much stuff going on that we had to tell them.

STEVE: The first journey [of] surrogacy was really easy. Then we tried a second one. We had a surrogate and three failed attempts. We used up all our embryos, and then we had to start over with a third. The second one, she had a miscarriage. We went through a lot of ups and downs. But we shared everything with our parents, and they were with us the whole way.

KENDALL: That's amazing. Many members of the gay community have challenging histories with their own families. When guys come out, there can be a major disconnect with their families, but if they still want to have kids, what can they do? What advice would you give them, as far as support?

MARK: I think they would need to feel comfortable with themselves. You need to be comfortable enough to be in good contact with your family, but you have to be comfortable with yourself before you start.

STEVE: I had always wanted, from a very, very young age, to have kids. I had a lot of internalized homophobia. I thought it was off the table, but I wanted to have a family, and I didn't think it was possible. I came out late.

I didn't think my parents were sending the right signals growing up, that they were truly accepting. But ultimately, they were very accepting. They didn't reject me when I came out. When I finally did, they were there for me. Then I met Mark. It certainly would not have been the right choice at that moment to have kids. We would have to grow and accept ourselves.

MARK: Me too. My father passed away when I was sixteen [years old] from AIDS, and he was gay also. I didn't want to be gay because I thought it was a death sentence for myself. But until I figured out that I was not going to die, my family accepted me for who I am, and I just wasn't ready to have kids. Then I met Steve, and we talked about family again.

KENDALL: So it's really about getting a foundation for yourself first before you go to that next step?

STEVE: I think both us felt a little bit alienated with our families. I didn't feel connected with my father. Mark had his father come out when he was very young and sort of left the family, so we both had father issues and stuff like that. I think we both wanted a family. You have to reconcile who you are as yourself, and then what ultimately you want in terms of family. There's a lot of self-development that needs to take place.

MARK: Right. You need to be more comfortable with yourself before you go into the next step, because it's quite a process to come out.

STEVE: It's easier for kids now.

MARK: Yeah, easier for them, because the parents are more accepting.

STEVE: Some.

KENDALL: Part of this book is about kids who go through estrangement and divorce, and how you get your act together before you become a dad. That's a core focus, so that's great advice. To that point, as that community grows, what would you recommend for gay couples? Are there resources online, other books to read that kind of inspired you? What's their next immediate step to get support?

STEVE: As you said, there are more and more people that are gay dads and having families. There are organizations.

MARK: Men having babies.

STEVE: Men having babies, which is how we first got involved. Surrogacy seminars, and things like that, [are] where you can learn about it. We're on Facebook [and] in a gay fathers' group. There are a ton of posts every single day.

PART 12

# Your Legacy

# CHAPTER 126

# Section Preview: Your Legacy

**B**esides my mother, I was blessed to have another strong-willed woman in my life who had a major influence on how I define family—my grandmother, Charlotte. She passed away at age ninety-four, but she lived independently until the age of ninety two.

Did I mention she lived in a three-story brownstone? "Strong-willed" may be an understatement. She was tough as nails, but also compassionate. She came of age during the Great Depression. Her husband fought the Nazis in World War Two, and when he came home, their daughter (my mother) was already three years old.

My mother was raised in Forest Hills, New York, which was a beautiful community and the perfect setting for my mother to grow up in the 1950s. It is still a fantastic little village in the city of New York.

The brownstone my grandmother lived in was a home of her choosing, and a residence she afforded from a thrifty lifestyle. Her husband, my grandfather, had no interest in buying a single-family home, given the work and upkeep it would entail, yet she was determined to provide a better life for her children, and she did not let gender bias in the banking community stop her. Despite being a stay-at-home mother with no income to speak of, she secured a mortgage and a deed on her own volition.

When I visited my grandmother's home as I grew up, it was a magical place for me to explore. The home was three stories tall, so every time I came, I found something new in all the nooks and crannies. Oh, the things I found!

A BB gun in the original box that was given to my uncle when he was a child; a train set from the 1950s; items from my grandfather's service in World War Two (like a sword!). My uncle earned two advanced collegiate degrees and loved to tinker with scientific stuff, which I also readily found in my grandmother's home. He was a child of the '60s, so (of course) he had a lava lamp he'd left at the home, which fascinated me.

Although my grandmother's strong will remained, her physical abilities to climb the stairs and take care of herself did not, so, after years of trying, my mother finally convinced her in 2005 to sell the home and move in with her in the suburbs of New Jersey. The move to her daughter's home was good for her, a blessing for her last few years to spend them with her best friend—my mother.

One of the chapters in this section suggests starting an heirloom box, a keepsake of items to pass down from one generation to the next. My heirloom box is an intricately designed wood inlay box my grandfather brought back from Germany after the war. When my grandmother passed, I found another similar box and started a collection of items that were meaningful to me. When that collection could no longer be contained to just two boxes, I started a third.

Today I have several treasures to pass down to my son. They will never be thrown away. He'll have items that go back to the 1920s, including the wedding rings that belonged to his great-great-grandparents and a Polish/English dictionary they used when they immigrated to the United States. These items have meaning, but more importantly, each item represents a story about family.

I've also drafted letters to my son in case something happens to me. They present some of life's lessons I want to pass down to him. I've instructed my wife to give each one to him at certain ages.

No matter where you come from, you can convey the importance of family in a number of ways. You can start your own traditions and share items or stories from previous generations that exude the value of their sacrifices and heritage.

Most importantly, you can represent a father with a purpose who espouses the importance of family to your children. If your father was not there to do this for you, it means you're stepping up and raising the bar for future generations.

What a wonderful way to be remembered.

# CHAPTER 127

# The Legacy of Your Fatherhood

This chapter is an exercise that will result in an ego trip of heightened proportions. But it touches on many topics already addressed in this book. If you follow the provided advice, you'll likely be on your way to becoming a great dad. That's the whole point of this work—to be a better parent to the next generation.

There's only one thing to focus on when it comes to establishing your legacy: **communication**. Your ability to communicate will make you a better husband and family member, a better employee (or leader) in a company, and a better dad. It's not about collecting material things, keeping up with the Joneses, or climbing the corporate ladder. That's all window dressing. One of the most important skills to focus on is your ability to communicate your feelings, hopes, and desires *in a meaningful way*.

Those who communicate succinctly and persuasively have an advantage over those who do not. It's common sense. If you can't articulate your thoughts so that someone clearly understands you, how will your daughter perceive you as she matures?

Think about her teenage years down the road. Practicing solid communication skills now with your family will give you a better chance to break through to her when it really counts. She's not going to listen to you all the time when she's a teenager, when she will be most susceptible to bad decisions and influences.

Your father/daughter relationship is a critical one. It will define how she will perceive men—and a potential spouse—for the rest of her life. Set the right tone and perception by communicating with her in an honest manner.

If you have a son, he will inevitably look to you for direction and define himself (on some level) by the code of conduct you espouse. Your ability to communicate will help maximize your son's ability to do the same, which will bode well for him later in life.

Every strong family, long-standing marriage, and meaningful parent/child relationship is anchored in active communication.

Isn't that a great way to be remembered?

# CHAPTER 128

# The Next Generation: Aim for a +1 Net Positive

At the very least, set a goal for your child to become a productive member of society.

Your daughter may not be able to walk yet, but if there's one thing to keep in mind over the course of her life, make sure she's productive. She may not re-invent space travel or cure cancer, but if you espouse a hard work ethic and sense of pride from a job well done, it will carry her very far.

Some people in society will always look for shortcuts or a quick hit, and they often espouse a sense of entitlement—a belief that the world owes them something. Others believe their place in the world is linear, the game is fixed, and they are held back by higher powers, thus they make little effort to better themselves. In truth, your child owes the world a certain level of gratitude just for being here, for having the opportunity to enjoy life, and the chance to make something of herself.

If your daughter wants to change careers later in life, will she blame others for having failed (if she does), or will she seek another degree to merit the change? Will she blame the costs of living on her inability to advance herself, or will she get a second job, cut back on expenses, and save to afford the changes she wants to make? Will she always need others to tell her how well she is performing, or will she have the self-confidence to know when she's done a good job and assess her own success?

Think about the lessons you can pass on to her to help her understand that her contribution truly matters. If you succeed, you'll have a lot less to worry about as she matures into a young woman.

In other words, raise a winner.

# CHAPTER 129

# The Envelope, Please

**Y**ou have a lot more "life" in your house as of late, or if you're expecting, it's about to explode in activity, involvement, and excitement.

You have a lot to look forward to. You have many lessons to pass along to your son when he starts to grow up. Here's something to consider: What critical life lessons would you like to pass along if you're not in the picture?

You're likely far removed in years and thought when it comes to your own demise, but like taxes, it is going to happen. It may seem a morbid subject that has no place in a book about infants and toddlers; however, what if you're not there in five, ten, or fifteen years' time to share the critical wisdom you've garnered? Are there important lessons you hope to pass along to give your son an advantage, or advice about what mistakes you may have made?

A terrific movie came out back in the 1990s called *My Life*, starring Michael Keaton and Nicole Kidman. The soon-to-be father made videos for his unborn son, and he did so because he was diagnosed with terminal cancer. The videos he made share short segments about the lessons he wanted to pass along to his child.

Maybe video is not your thing, so here's an alternative: Write four separate letters for different stages of your child's development. Don't worry about the length, typos, or grammatical errors. Draft a letter for different developmental stages (that you believe are critical) and make sure your spouse knows what you're planning.

Maybe one is about your mother and the relationship you had with her, how important it was, and your wish for your son to treat your wife with the same level of respect and care. Another could be when he is about to enter high school, so write about your experiences and the advice you would give him. Write about his first job, first "A" in school, perhaps major achievements later in his life. Share your heart and don't let anyone read the letters. Most of all, be honest about what you write—good or bad.

Then put each letter in a separate envelope; if you can, seal each closed with wax so your son will know it's never been opened. This is for his eyes only. It might seem dramatic, but he'll know you took the trouble to ensure direct communication with him after you're gone, without any filter. Tell your wife to place them in a fire-proof box or within your security deposit box at the bank, and instruct her to share each letter when the time is right. Make sure to mark each envelope for each occasion or life event.

Those four envelopes ensure you'll pass along important wisdom, which may help to enhance important moments throughout your son's life. This dovetails into the next chapter and the most critical thing you can do as a successful father.

And that is to establish a legacy.

# CHAPTER 130

# The Heirloom Box

During World War Two, my grandfather served in the Army's Seventh and Eighth Armored Divisions. He saw action in the European theatre and, according to my grandmother, his wartime experiences affected him for the remainder of his life. After he passed away, she recalled the harrowing nightmares he endured for decades, the result of post-traumatic stress disorder (PTSD).

While my grandfather served overseas, he procured a number of items he later brought home with him. The most valuable was a German Luger handgun (unbeknownst to my grandma for a long time, who was terrified of guns). This particular item was worth thousands of dollars. Upon his death, she found the Luger and promptly dropped it off at a local Veterans of Foreign Wars (VFW) office to get rid of it. For years, our family chastised her for doing so. Most upsetting to me was the fact that I missed the chance to procure a true piece of history. German Lugers represent an extremely rare wartime keepsake.

My grandfather also brought home a number of wooden boxes, intricately detailed with wood inlays that showcase German castles. The level of detail and wood grains are exquisitely hand-crafted. They are small, perhaps 12 x 19 x 6 inches. I appreciated them at a young age. I started filling one that my grandmother gave me and called it my "heirloom box." Other boxes were handed down to me in the years that followed.

One item I added to my heirloom box was a pair of German

binoculars. When given to me, I wondered if my grandpa picked them up off a battlefield somewhere in Europe. The binoculars will remain safe in my box until my son is old enough to appreciate the story behind them.

With one box filled, I started filling other boxes that were handed down to me: my father's passports from the 1960s, which highlight his global travels; his desk nameplate from the job he had for years at Chase Manhattan Bank in New York City; a blue tiepin my mom gave me before my high school graduation; my grandfather's "U.S." lapel pins from his Army dress uniform; a single dollar bill from the 1920s given to me by my grandmother; and rare coins and silver dollars from my uncle.

I also added things from my own upbringing that meant something to me. One of my most treasured keepsakes is a small, fake skeleton necklace with a glass diamond in one eye. My mom and dad gave it to me when I was seven or eight during a trip to Disney World, the last vacation we took together as a family before my parents officially divorced.

Then I started to add items that related to my experiences with my son. One was a small container of sand, taken from the beach where we took him as a newborn shortly after his adoption was finalized. We placed his tiny feet in the sand and watched a beautiful sunset together. I later scooped up the sand, which is now saved in an heirloom box, along with letters I've written (and sealed with wax) for him to receive at certain times in his life.

When we were reorganizing our storage closets, I put the heirloom boxes side-by-side and took account of what I had collected. It was amazing to see so many wonderful memories and artifacts in one place. I sorted the items so that each box holds related contents and tells a particular story—all stories I will pass down to my son.

Taking the time to do all of this provided me with a unique perspective. Despite having an estranged relationship with my father, the keepsakes the boxes contain go back to my great grandfather and represent nearly one hundred years of family history. This depth of history represents a meaningful legacy I can share with my son, which he will hopefully one day share with his own kids.

This process also provides one with a generational perspective. No matter where you netted out with your dad, good or bad, you still have sweet and wonderful memories to share with your children. They connect and showcase how far families can take us. From an immigrant voyage across the sea, to the launch of a successful business, to military service to one's country, these stories represent family treasures.

What can you find from your family's history to pass along? If you can think of or locate a few items, find something cool to put them in and save it. And when your children are older, make it an annual event to bring out the keepsakes and share the valuable stories they hold.

If you can, pass along a family legacy that extends long before you were born. Think how meaningful it will be for the generations that follow.

# CHAPTER 131

# Final Thoughts

**I**have one last piece of advice to share, and I hope you never forget it.

*You are going to make mistakes as a father.* As I noted in a previous chapter, babies do not come with instruction manuals. You learn as you go. Advice is given, considered, and either accepted or rejected, depending on your point of view. The point of this book is to provide some basic concepts of how to parent, but the ultimate judgment about whether you've made a wise and correct decision belongs to you.

If not . . . **course correct and adapt**. The idea of failing as a parent can only happen in one of two ways. Number one: You do not learn from your mistakes and continue to repeat the same pattern of behavior. If you believe the same repetitive pattern will result in a different outcome, doctors have a definition for it—insanity. The worst decision you can make is not admitting you made a mistake. If that's a private conclusion, reach out to others (your wife, then your friends) and discuss it. Bounce your concerns off of them. Maybe you're being too hard on yourself! There's nothing wrong with setting long-term goals as a parent with regard to the structure or values you wish to espouse. That represents the end game. But when it comes to the "means," take a fluid approach when it comes to hitting those goals. The result will make you a better dad.

The second way to fail as a parent? Not showing up. Not being there when your wife and kids need you. Being a constant in the life of your child pays enormous dividends.

But I don't have to tell you any more about this last point. You bought this book for a reason. My hope is you and I share the same ambition, and that is to provide a better life for our children compared to what we had when we were kids. It's a simple goal, but why so many men fail to live up to the challenge is a mystery. That can change.

And it starts with us.

Volume #2 of *Rookie Father* is already in the works, and it will focus on the toddler years. You'll find my email on the "Contact the Author" page at the back of this book. Reach out to me, if you'd like. Tell me what resonated with you or what didn't. Any and all feedback is welcome. I've espoused the value of constructive criticism in this book, and I live by it.

I wish you and your family good health and happiness in the years to come.

Sincerely,

**Kendall Smith**

# Contact the Author

Invite you to get in touch, share some feedback, and join a community of fathers who are doing everything they can to provide a better experience for their kids.

We've all heard that old African proverb that teaches it takes a village to raise a child. You are not alone in your desire to provide your child with a healthy and happy upbringing. You can contact me directly at TheRookieFather@gmail.com.

For additional content and ideas, visit the *Rookie Father* website at www.TheRookieFather.com.

**Social Connections**
Facebook: https://www.facebook.com/TheRookieFather
Instagram: www.instagram.com/therookiefather/
Twitter: Handle = https://twitter.com/RookieFather

# About the Author

**K**endall Smith lives in New Jersey and has been married to his wife, Allison, for nearly sixteen years. Together, they have a seven-year-old son named Connor. Kendall works during the day in the digital marketing industry and during the early morning hours as an author. His literary works cover a range of subject matters, including the thriller *Vault 21-12* (Percussion Publishing, 2015). He's also worked for notable publications in the past, such as *Wired* and *Men's Health* magazines.

Much like the readers of *Rookie Father*, Kendall also grew up without a regular father figure during his childhood. His parents separated when he was six years old, at which point he shared a long-distance relationship with his father. Fortunately, his mother's love and the support of other relatives helped provide him with a strong family structure. During his youth, he observed and appreciated the influence of other fathers in the community. He now leads by example, sharing the lessons he's learned from role models within and outside of his family, in order to provide his son with a sense of love and security.

# About Familius

## Visit Our Website: www.familius.com

Familius is a global trade publishing company that publishes books and other content to help families be happy. We believe that the family is the fundamental unit of society and that happy families are the foundation of a happy life. We recognize that every family looks different, and we passionately believe in helping all families find greater joy. To that end, we publish books for children and adults that invite families to live the Familius Ten Habits of Happy Families: *love together, play together, learn together, work together, talk together, heal together, read together, eat together, give together* and *laugh together*. Founded in 2012, Familius is located in Sanger, California.

## Connect

Facebook: www.facebook.com/familiustalk
Twitter: @familiustalk, @paterfamilius1
Pinterest: www.pinterest.com/familius
Instagram: @familiustalk

FAMILIUS

THE MOST IMPORTANT WORK YOU EVER
DO WILL BE WITHIN THE WALLS OF
YOUR OWN HOME.